The Metanoia Factor

(met-ah-noy-ah)

Controlling Destiny

...Getting What you Want While Making a Difference

By Dr. Ty Talcott and Dr. Scott Elliott

The Metanoia Factor: Controlling Destiny: Getting What You Want While Making a Difference

Published by Hats Off Books™
610 East Delano Street, Suite 104, Tucson, Arizona 85705 U.S.A.
www.hatsoffbooks.com

International Standard Book Number: 1-58736-443-3
Library of Congress Control Number: 2005920250

Cynthia Richardson

Cover photo and graphics by Cynthia Richardson

When your project deserves the best call "The Cover Girl"™
Phone: (972) 771-2079
Online: www.studioc.biz
Email: Cynthia@studioc.biz
Studio "C" provides the best in digital graphics, portraiture, and special occasion coverage.

ACKNOWLEDGMENTS

We are taking this opportunity to thank our families, who stand beside us in our brilliance and craziness; our most prized friends and business associates, who are members of our Inner Circle; and all the mentors in our lives, who have made mistakes so we won't have to repeat them. We only hope we can be as important in the lives of others as we move forward on our mission to significantly impact the lives of one million people.

Thank you

The late Dr. Rolla Pennell
Ila Calton
Roger Calton
Janice Schoen
Jon Templeton
V.K. Gupta
Bud Inman
Randy Winski
Brian Eberstien
Gary Ryan Blair (The Goals Guy)
Gordon Anderson
Kenny Bounds
David Bertrand
Jana Mitchum

Travis Bond
Dr. Jimmy Gutman
Dr. Mike Martin
Carl Kleimann
David Rettig
Jason Jones
Gary Banwart
Patte Kent
Dr. J.P. Johnson
Dr. Dale White
Dr. Bobby Hollander
Dr. Kevin Raef
Joel Godfrey
Dr. Bill Quain
Dr. Roy Hillgartner

And so many more of the greatest teachers in the world!

This book is dedicated to you if you are ready to take action and go to the next level in your life—whatever that might be.

TABLE OF CONTENTS

FORWARD

Have you ever had a thought that instantly changed the way you viewed a situation?

The "light bulb" flashed on? The "aha" occurred? You experienced a "metanoia."

There is no truer sense of understanding or clarity. This is more than your intellect kicking in to allow you to better understand a situation, and it is bigger than your belief systems. This is a personal paradigm shift—your life just changed. It is impossible to return to the old thought process, as you are wiser and see things from a new perspective. Many times you will wonder how you ever saw things the "old" way.

Although some metanoias seem minor, these transitions in thought process result in high-impact changes.

In fact, a metanoia can be the start of a whole new life!

These "instant" thought transitions are, in fact, not instant at all. They are a result of a lifetime of learning and experience that brings you to the point where the "aha" occurs. All of your thoughts, experiences, and learning instantly combine to form a new awareness. You see things in a brand new light.

When you take this new perspective and apply it in your daily life, you have just engaged the "metanoia factor."

THE METANOIA FACTOR

Metanoia Factor = the advantages brought to your life from accelerated achievement of personal objectives due to applying these instant-thought transmutations (metanoias) to daily living.

This process of recognition and application allows for mental clarity while simultaneously attracting the necessary people and resources to live a life of prosperity and peace. Life enhancements begin to magically appear.

This book will provide you the necessary information, insight, and methods to create the essential mental environment for metanoias to strike!

As you proceed and grasp the magnificent power of *The Metanoia Factor*, you will not just think differently—you will actually be different. You will enjoy new paths to personal prosperity and peace.

Bring on the metanoias!

INTRODUCTION

Combine the right mental attitude with the right team and victory is yours.

Today we are going to start an exciting and prosperous journey together.

This book will assist you with the subject nearest and dearest to your heart—getting what you desire from life.

You will be guided through the maze of how to accomplish your desires in ways that simultaneously benefit mankind, thus leaving a better world for generations to come.

> Is this book for you? Yes!
> Will this book benefit your family? Yes!
> Your friends? Yes!
> Your career? Yes!
> The world? Yes!

It is hard to think of any project that would hold your attention, elicit your actions, and create more natural motivation than learning how to get what you want out of life.

What could be more important?

What could be more exciting?

Most of us blindly "work" on getting what we want every single day. However, the reality is that few of us ever experience the achievement of our desires. Many of us don't even know what it is we truly want from this life. What is it that would provide a sense of prosperity, happiness, and fulfillment?

Achieving what you want in life involves several stages. Each stage is critical to the end result. Life is fun again when you evolve to the point of waking every morning knowing what you are going after in life, how to get it, and how to utilize "the science of applied motivation" to create the energy necessary to carry you to a successful completion.

A huge part of successfully attaining your personal desires depends on developing a team to assist you. There are very few worthwhile objectives you can achieve alone. Developing an efficient, trustworthy team will skyrocket your rate and level of success. The number one reason individuals and businesses fail to reach their objectives is because they fail to surround themselves with the "right" people.

Somehow, large corporations have learned this golden rule, hence their massive success. This proven team factor rarely filters down to small business and individuals. When Henry Ford was complimented on his brilliance, he said his only brilliance was surrounding himself with the right people.

Whether you apply this rule to sports, family, business groups, or organizations, developing a solidified team with definitive communication systems and a clearly understood objective is essential to success. We call this a "power team." Communication and clarity of objective are the keys to success.

The best way to create a power team is to strengthen the individual links by assisting each person on the team to learn the skills required for personal success. This process increases every team member's personal excitement level, as well as their willingness to assist others.

A fact of life is the following: We all wear a two-sided rotating sign on our foreheads. One side states, "I'm important." The other side asks, "What's in it for me?" Unless you address these two issues with every single person you meet in life, your ability to maximize relationships will be limited. You will never acquire the level of assistance and support that is available to you.

The unique approach of building a power team allows business owners to achieve significantly higher financial returns and increased efficiency. Transforming standard employees from "task-doers" into a united power team has massive positive impact on productivity and decreases turnover. Our company, Power Strategies Incorporated, provides unique customized seminars to assist businesses and individuals in accomplishing this essential task.

While this book is about you, it is evident that you require others to accomplish your goals and dreams. The most obvious people to assist in your new path to higher achievement are friends, family, coworkers, and business partners. Each of these individuals possesses an unparalleled ability to accelerate your achievements. Remember, communication is key. We will discuss the importance of clear communication multiple times throughout this book. Like minds are synergistic and bring about amazing results.

Personally experiencing high levels of success, then passing this information, knowledge, and experience along to others who have the proper mindset to accept and apply this information will allow you to achieve everything you want in life while making a significant positive impact on the world in which we live.

There are two areas of life where power teams are essential:
Business
Family

Your family power team should never be overlooked. When spouses, parents, and children all understand and participate in common objectives, with each member having an ultimate benefit, you will be amazed at how much can be accomplished.

To start this process we are going to teach you how to create the future you have always desired. As well, we hope we have the opportunity to teach your family, friends, partners, employees, and coworkers these same valuable lessons.

We are going to take you on a journey that will lead to success. We will accomplish this through teaching specific information and techniques, such as:

~ How to clearly define what you want from life
~ How to benefit by functioning like society's top 20 percent while breaking free of your comfort zone.
~ How to utilize higher thought processes in order to work smarter, not harder
~ How to control your thoughts and focus your energy to create essential self-motivation
~ How to overcome detrimental fears and self-doubt
~ How to turn a plan into a result
~ The advantages of and how to create power teams

Would you like for us to teach you these principles and methods? If so, this book is for you. If applied, each page will result in a major positive impact on your life. However, our teaching is only a piece of the puzzle. You must be willing to apply this information to your daily life in order to create the results you desire. You are the only one controlling your destiny!

Are you ready? Of course you are, otherwise you would have stopped reading already!

Interestingly, we are now the newest members of your personal power team. We'll be here to guide and support you every step of the way. By working together we can help you accomplish your personal goals to live a healthier, happier, and more abundant life. You will become closer to your family, friends, and coworkers as you apply the information and techniques outlined in the chapters ahead.

During the course of this book, we will drill a deep and productive oil well within your conscious and subconscious mind. Some of you will choose to put a small pump on the well and only receive a trickle of insight and productive change; others will hook up a huge pump and suck out every bit possible—once again, you are in control of your destiny.

We will take an in-depth look into your innermost thoughts and belief systems. This is essential in order to maximize your personal results and create positive change.

We feel it is essential to clarify that we are not going to enter the arena of religion or spirituality. While these are critical areas in one's life, they involve characteristics outside the scope of these teachings. We will focus all of our teachings on factors that are 100 percent within our control and, therefore, within our ability to change.

You will receive guidance in clarifying your purpose and objectives. By clarifying and understanding your purpose and objectives, you can recognize the methods and techniques that best apply to your situation.

The science of applied motivation will maximize the use of your mind and body to accomplish your desires, while making a positive difference in the world around you.

Do you truly want to do something special with your life? Do you want to make a significant positive impact on those around you? Your daily actions have an immense impact on the entire universe. Only you can ultimately choose the mark you will leave behind. Will people remember you for the many accomplishments you made and how those accomplishments affected results in the world around you? Are you leaving positive or negative impacts on a daily basis?

Mark Victor Hansen, of *Chicken Soup for the Soul* fame, refers to the "butterfly effect." One butterfly flapping its wings combines with all forces of nature to create wind patterns around the world. Without the butterfly, the pattern changes.

Remember the movie *It's a Wonderful Life* with Jimmy Stewart. He thought he had no impact on the world, only to find that had he not existed, the world would have been a very different place.

When he changed his belief about his importance and contribution to the world, he changed the way he acted. When he changed the way he acted, he altered what he got back from the universe.

The key factor is this: whether you believe your actions alter the world around you is irrelevant; they do. There is no changing this fact. To accomplish more in life and have a more positive impact on those around you, you must internalize and implement the synergistic universal power strategies outlined in this book. Like gravity—they just work.

We are going to have an incredible journey together, revealing insights and methods allowing you to utilize these forces and change your life while making a positive impact along the way.

Today's society has fallen under the misconception that we have little or no control over our lives. This is simply not true. We have a tremendous amount of control, and there are massive opportunities to create the futures we desire. We will not only prove this to you, but will also provide you the new skills necessary to create the life you have always wanted to live.

Take the time to apply each lesson to your personal life.

Remember: Think. Then plan. Then act.

The Japanese have accused Americans of following a business and life methodology of "ready—fire—aim." For the majority of our society this is all too accurate.

Let's immediately begin to "think—plan—act." This will result in a life you will love. We only have one chance on this planet. Most spend their lives never accomplishing what is within their potential. Every second counts.

Let's get started!

METANOIA FACTOR 1:

Your life is guided by emotions— not intellect

Understanding how to control your destiny is essential for accomplishing higher levels of personal achievement.

Unfortunately, the majority of individuals never take the time to learn how to control life-changing factors that are directly within their control. People feel their lives are guided by their intellect, when in fact, very little intellect is utilized. We actually live the majority of our lives based on our emotional responses. Emotions are the only true underlying motivators for action, and emotions are controlled by beliefs.

Let us illustrate. When you were young someone told you that you should act a certain way. You believed them. Since it is the way you believe you *should* act, you feel guilty when you don't act the "correct" way. Most of us therefore act according to how we feel we *should* act in order to avoid the guilt created by our current belief system. You act because of emotion.

Your actions are generally determined by your strongest emotional response. If someone states you *should* act in a certain manner, you will act this way if your guilt outweighs your desire to act differently. On the other hand, if your emotion of guilt is not strong, you will act in the manner that provides you a high emotional return—happiness or satisfaction. If you know you should not eat that ice cream cone, but the emotional desire is very high, you will eat it and gain the momentary emotional and sensory delight...and bear the guilt.

You did not enjoy the taste with your intellect.

The large majority of our "shoulds" are developed very early in life. As children we possess very little intellectual development or life experience on which to base our acceptance or rejection of the shoulds with which we are presented. This is critical to understand, because you act according to many shoulds that you have never analyzed as an adult with your expanded intellect and experience.

Are you living by *your* shoulds, or are you living by the shoulds of your parents or others? Have you taken the time to decipher whether or not you truly believe in your current beliefs? Is the belief system you live by actually yours—or does it belong to someone else?

As an example, most of us heard statements like these when we were young:

"You aren't the center of the universe, you know!"
"The world doesn't revolve around you!"
"There are other people to think about too!"

The intention of these early "mentors" may have been well-meaning (to get you to share your toys, or pitch in and help so they wouldn't kick you out of kindergarten the very first day), however, the method used may have left a failure mechanism in place that is robbing you of getting what you want from life and keeping you from making a true difference in the world.

The need of parents and teachers to accelerate the process of sharing, ahead of our ability to understand why we would *want* to share, sets many of us up for a life of lack.

For the rest of our lives we constantly judge whether acts are *selfless* or *selfish*. Then we either feel guilty about performing selfish actions or take no action at all.

During those young ages we don't have the experience to realize "what's in it for us" when we share or pitch in. Nor do we realize how those activities are, in and of themselves, *selfish* acts.

Hopefully, later in life, we realize by working together (pitching in) and pooling resources (sharing) everyone gets more. Then we understand "what's in it for us."

It is our opinion that there are no selfless acts.

This may be a foreign concept to you and difficult to fully grasp. Once understood however, it is a truly freeing revelation.

First, every act is selfish. There is nothing wrong with this fact. You do what you do because you want one of the following outcomes:

a. You want the desired benefit gained by your action (obviously centered on your wants).

b. It makes you feel good (the reason you do charity work, take pride in your children, help others, etc.).

c. You want to avoid a consequence (i.e., don't want the "bad" feelings of being punished, failing, being criticized, etc.).

You think you "should" (i.e., you will feel guilty if you don't do the action, therefore you proceed in order to not feel guilty).

Since all of these produce a result you want, the action is selfish.

Second, with any and all actions in life you must ask yourself a critical question: is it working?

If it is working, keep doing it; if it is not, stop and do something different. This is the basis for all successful progression.

At first this may appear to lead to a society of no morals—far from it!

As just one example, let's look at the Judeo-Christian religion's Old Testament.

"THOU SHALT NOT KILL."

How does this work?

If we all ran around killing each other, how would our world be?

How safe would you feel?

How safe would you feel for your children?

If you were always afraid someone was going to kill you, how productive could you be, and how much of a difference could you make?

"THOU SHALL NOT STEAL."

How does this work?

We think it makes a better society than one where thievery is encouraged or rampant.

We are sure you get the idea.

Bottom line: following the commandments works, and if everyone did so, all the time, the world would work better.

This does not negate or minimize the tenets of any other religious belief—most of the major religions have tenets that, if followed, allow society to function at a higher level.

This book starts with society's moral rules—that work—then builds on these with synergistic universal power strategies that will accelerate your path in getting what you want while making a difference.

Let's proceed to Metanoia Factor #2!

Metanoia Factor 2

The way to have what you want is by "asking the right question"!

Have you ever had a situation arise where you felt you had little to no control? Many individuals spend their entire lives in this helpless mental state. "Asking the right question" provides you the needed control to make change and acquire your preferred result.

It is impossible to achieve your personal objectives and ambitions while allowing outside circumstances and individuals to control your life.

Do you ever find yourself asking *why* something happened *to* you? Do you ever blame others and ask *why* they *did* something *to* you?

Placing blame and playing the victim role results in total loss of personal control. It leaves you in a helpless state. Let us make one point crystal clear: if you want to maximize your achievements in life, you must immediately stop blaming others and accept 100 percent of the responsibility for where you are in life.

Once you have done this you can exert control to create positive change.

For many it is difficult to take this concept to the max. After all, how can you help it if your river raft trip was ruined because of rain? You can't control the rain!

But, in fact, it is still your responsibility. You chose to go rafting *that day*. You *chose* rafting over bowling—that would have been unaffected by weather. You *chose* to be upset the trip was called off. What if you didn't like rafting? You would be happy the trip was off, but you *chose* to enjoy rafting and you chose to *make it* a hobby.

Can you start to see how you play a role in everything that happens to you? One of the main ways you play a role is by the way you react to what happens in your daily life. It's not what is happening, it is how you feel about what is happening, that determines the quality of your life and your level of happiness.

Once you have experienced this metanoia (mental transition), you may feel more responsibility, but you will also feel a tremendous amount of freedom. All of a sudden there are endless possibilities for controlling your life! You are no longer a victim!

Let's face reality. We all play the victim role from time to time. It's *how long* you stay in this mode that's important.

To illustrate, Dr. Talcott will tell you about his duplexes.

Rental properties are supposed to make a positive cash flow, go up in value, and get paid off by someone else while you take the depreciation. That is how you make money in the rental real estate game.

I had several duplexes in my rental property corral that I was pretty happy with, and a management company that was taking care of them on my behalf. Life was wonderful.

I am sitting at home thinking I have a few thousand dollars a month in cash accumulating in the duplex account. Then I get a call from the management company saying I am five thousand dollars in the hole! To make matters worse, I am told rents are going down. I am also informed that one unit has been vacant for three months and all it has is a sign in the yard to advertise its vacancy because the *Dallas Morning News* rates went up and they can't afford to advertise anymore.

Did I go to "victim land"! You should have heard me yelling.

"Why didn't you inform me? Why did advertising rates increase? Are they idiots? Don't they understand that if they lowered the rates they would make tons more money in volume? Why can't you advertise as my management company anymore? You're trying to tell me that even though I pay you, I have to now market my own rental units? Why does the bank think it can continue to charge the interest rates these properties are financed at with current rates so low? Why do tenants think anyone can afford to run properties at these low rental rates? Why are all these people ganging up on me? Why is the sky blue and why doesn't the water turn to wine when I touch it?"

I was on a roll, yelling at the walls or whoever was on the phone.

Understand that in victim land, you have *zero* control.

I was suffering from the "why me?" phenomenon. The key is to recognize it and correct it immediately. How can you recognize the "why me?" phenomenon? Did you catch how many times I asked "why"?

When you are out of control you can't change anything.

Therefore, if you stay in that mode nothing changes and often you get stuck there, sometimes for the rest of your life.

Some people spend their whole lives asking "why me" and never accomplish anything of significance. To them, this is justified, because after all, nothing is ever the victim's fault! Someone else is to blame. But no matter who is at "fault," the reality is that if that person never changes, they never have what they want from life.

Their life is destined to stagnate until they begin "asking the right question." As soon as they stop asking "why me" and start asking "how," they begin down the road of personal control and recovery.

With regard to my duplexes, one of the "right" questions was: "How do I get these rental units back to positive cash flow?" As soon as I mentally asked that question, I instantly took back my ability to make change. I was no longer the helpless victim. I regained control.

Once I had the right question, I started asking everyone with whom I spoke. I would "ask" by first telling my story. I would describe my situation and say that I needed assistance.

About the fourth person I spoke with told me they had a relative in the property management business who still advertised in the *Dallas Morning News*. This got my attention. Long story short, I got a new property management company that charges less, has more experience, has their own construction crew, and doesn't charge add-on fees for fix up.

They got my properties leased—at increased rates—in about two weeks.

In fact, my old management company turned over the management of their other properties to my new guy!

Well, that was pretty cool, so I decided to keep speaking with everyone I came in contact with about how to maximize my properties even more.

I was speaking with a woman, who was a professional in residential lending, about a completely different topic. I decided to tell her my duplex story and ask her how I could maximize my return. She introduced me to an individual who ended up refinancing all my properties, including my home, at a much lower rate, which drastically reduced my monthly payments!

Well, this just kept getting better. So, I kept on pushing. What could it possibly hurt to continue sharing my story and asking my "how" question to individuals I met? Worst case scenario would be that they could not assist me. You never gain anything in life if you don't share what you're looking for.

My quest led to something I certainly never imagined while yelling on the telephone during my initial "victim" mode. As previously mentioned, Dr. Elliott and I own and operate a seminar/consulting firm. The main focus of our company is to "unleash human potential" for individuals. For businesses, we work directly with their employees and turn them into efficient power teams designed to allow each employee to achieve higher personal goals in such a way that the business achieves its objectives in the process. Our methods are unique and immensely effective.

Interested individual clients, from this large source of people from corporate contracts, are invited to join our elite "Inner Circle." The Inner Circle is specifically designed to assist individuals in taking their lives to the next level of personal and professional prosperity through proven forms of personal development, wealth accumulation, and asset protection. (It's been stated that your income will become the average of the five people you spend the most time with. We therefore surround ourselves with wealthy people and those who wish to become wealthy. The Inner Circle is powerful and available to all who are serious about developing a higher consciousness and more enjoyable standard of living. (The only thing that will alter the person you are today from the person you are five years from today are the books you read, the CDs you listen to, the events you attend, the people you meet, and the relationships you develop.) The Inner Circle provides unparalleled resources to maximize each of these critical areas for life enhancement. You may learn more details about the Inner Circle by going to http://www.appliedmotivation.net and clicking on "Individuals."

This group, our Inner Circle, had been asking how they could be involved in real estate. Well, we arranged to put our new property expert, finance expert, insurance folks, and the rest of the team required to effectively own rental properties in a room and asked them the right question: "How do we create a system where small investors can participate in real estate projects and/or own properties without having to learn what I had to learn and assemble the team I had to assemble—just put their money down and access a complete 'turnkey' system that works?" This group of seasoned professionals, from this one question, ultimately created the finest real estate investing program I have ever seen. All members of our Inner Circle group have access to this program. It's a convenient, secure method to create wealth while avoiding the many pitfalls that commonly afflict the inexperienced real estate investor. It also allows smaller investors to participate in "group" properties, thus providing them the ability to get their feet wet and slowly grow to larger levels of participation. The most exciting part is witnessing the powerful results of this system and what it's doing for so many financially. All this from asking the right question!

So what really is good news and what is bad news? Was the initial call I received informing me that the account was in the hole good news or bad news?

Remember this question and apply it to situations as they arise; it will help stop incorrect judgment of events in your life—who knows what's good news and what's bad news?

Our coauthor Billy Parker gives us a well-written illustration of how life can seem to have taken a bad turn but ultimately results in achieving your dream.

WHO KNOWS WHAT'S GOOD NEWS AND WHAT'S BAD NEWS

I thought I was about as happy as a man could be—an excellent marriage, three great kids, and a great career. I was a thirty-six-year-old MD-80 captain for American Airlines based in Dallas/Fort Worth, Texas, and a pilot instructor at the flight academy (an honor offered to less than one out of two hundred pilots).

Billy Parker

Then September 11 occurred. That was a black day in American history and also devastating to the airline industry. I lost my position as an instructor immediately. By the end of 2002, my income was drastically reduced. And then the real hammer dropped.

My choice was to commute to the East Coast as a captain or stay in Dallas/Fort Worth as a lower-paid copilot.

I chose to stay, refusing to be an absentee husband and father. But how does a person deal with so much bad news? I was praying for a change, and I was ready to take action.

God identifies those ready to act on the opportunities he offers, and my prayers were soon answered.

During my life I had gone through the trauma of buying a new home. What a bad experience that was! I saw a need for a better way. Typically the best opportunities in life are those when you clearly see a need and fill it.

While interest rates were at an all-time low and the refinance boom was in full swing, people were still overwhelmed by the process of a major purchase. What if there were a way to underpromise and overdeliver while focusing on customer satisfaction, and help walk people through the process? Certainly people would appreciate that and refer others! In fact, homebuilders, CPAs, realtors, and financial planners should want a service to take the mystery out of the mortgage process for their clients and customers.

In May of 2003, I took a position with Old Capital, Residential Lending for just that purpose.

I knew instantly that Internet lenders were some of my best friends, as that industry produced thousands of dissatisfied customers looking for an alternative.

These lenders simply advertise low rates and low closing costs. Unsuspecting individuals jump in quickly, not realizing they don't have all the options. Many first-time buyers are unaware how complex the lending process is and find out, only too late, that internet lenders provide no real, live person to keep up with the details and make sure the process is painless, efficient, and on-time. In fact, all too often borrowers end up finding they made a poor decision.

If the borrowers had only worked with a professional, they could have evaluated all the rate and term sheets, as well as hundreds of customized options.

I am that professional. I treat my customers like my airline passengers: get them there safely and on time.

Giving clients a guided tour through the loan process is the best way for them to know what to expect, to be realistic, and to reduce stress.

I found with Old Capital I was able to do just that.

The company and I have the same philosophies, and they have the programs to back up the philosophy. They believe in "Deliver + 1" (Ken Blanchard and Sheldon Bowles of Raving Fans)—try to improve on every loan by 1 percent while delivering the loan on time and meeting clients' expectations.

They have put together over seventy lenders and literally hundreds of loan products to meet clients' needs and maximize their cash flow. This is accomplished through diagnostic questions that reveal the short- and long-term goals of customers so that they can be matched to the correct loan program.

With the strong backing of Old Capital I was free to add my own special touches, such as making sure clients receive a copy of their credit report, teaching them how to evaluate and track loan settlement charges for accuracy, getting them their settlement statement forty-eight hours ahead of closing to spot "hiccups," and assuring them I will personally attend the closing to make sure all goes as anticipated. I also include post-closing surveys to evaluate my performance and continue my relationship with clients via educational newsletters.

The only piece left to the puzzle was to find borrowers in need of my service. I decided to do this by establishing relationships with the people who know the borrowers.

I formed relationships with realtors to prequalify their clients so they didn't waste time shopping "too much house." I created relationships with homebuilders by creating property profiles and sharing the cost of bulk mailers. I won over CPAs and financial planners by helping them maximize savings and cash flow for their clients so they could apply the funds to other investments, such as 401(k)s, SEPs, or 529 educational funds.

The result? When a need meets a solution, it creates a successful change of careers! What a difference spotting a need and going for it can make. Waking every morning at home with my wife and three children and setting out to bring someone's dream into reality is truly a blessed life.

Now, it is music to my ears hearing the new owners breathe a sigh of relief and say, "That went well," and it warms my heart seeing their excitement as they buy their first home.

Who knows what's good news and what's bad news?

Billy Parker
Phone: (817) 821-9533
E-mail: bparker@ocrl.com

CB∞CB

Circumstances can seem overwhelming, but once you set out to accomplish your goals and desires, and you stop allowing circumstances or other individuals to control your life, you become 100 percent responsible for your actions. At that point you have the mental control needed to succeed.

We know what separates successful people from unsuccessful people. It's not luck. It's not a degree. It's not their age or how cute they are. It's their mindset, the beliefs and the principles they live by!

Wrong mindset = failure.

Right mindset = success!

Once you have an unbeatable mindset resulting in more stable relationships, self-worth, peacefulness, security, flexibility, confidence, and success consciousness, you quickly break the "why me" phenomenon that is responsible for blocking your ability to develop the lifestyle you truly desire.

Here's the decision you need to make:

Continue asking "why" things happen *to you*,
or
ask "how" to make things happen the way you want them to be.

Make this mental shift and regain control by asking the right question.

Everyone always wants to know how to change. Here is an exercise that will assist you in doing so. This exercise will also allow you to come to a new awareness of your innermost belief systems. Many of your beliefs may, in fact, be based on untruths or partial truths. Once these are revealed, they will no longer hold the power to stagnate your life. Once revealed a lie has no power.

You will only accomplish this with the right attitude. An appropriate attitude about your life situation, reasonable plans to move forward, and a healthy dose of confidence will win every time.

You can have everything going for you, have a bad attitude, and fail. On the other hand, you can have nothing going for you with the entire deck stacked against you, have a winning attitude and succeed.

You need to change your mindset to change your reality. Gaining control of your thought patterns will allow you to alter your actions, which in turn results in a drastically different outcome.

So let's take action. Nothing happens without doing something!

Step 1: List all areas of your life where you want to achieve more.

Example: I need to spend more time with my children.

Step 2: Create the right "how" question that, if answered, would solve your situation.

Example: How can I utilize my time more efficiently in order to set aside quality time each day to spend with my children?

Step 3: Repeat this question over and over again to yourself, and also be sure to share this question with everyone with whom you come in contact.

If you want change, take control.

Remember, victims never want their problems solved. We are all surrounded by individuals who play the victim role each and every day. Don't allow them to control your life! They want to monopolize your precious time with their endless problems. When this occurs—and we guarantee it will—simply say: "I understand your problem. Let me ask you this. How do you want it to be and what are you going to do about it?"

At best you will get an answer like, "I don't know, I just know I don't want it to be like this!"

This will typically end the conversation and allow you to resume a productive life instead of listening to their endless problems.

Remember, if you are complaining about how it is but don't know how you want it to be, how will you ever know when you have it like you want it?

Figure out how you want it to be by asking the right "how" question and make sure you ask experts in the area, as well as the people you see on a daily basis. Again, the only things that make you a different person are the books you read, CDs you listen to, events you attend, and the people you meet.

Our coauthor Fred Van Liew can give us some insight to the power of mentors.

BOOKS, DREAMS, ACTION,
AND A SECRET WEAPON

Fred Van Liew

I look out a across the audience. Over four thousand people are giving me a standing ovation! All I did was tell them about my water and air purification systems and how they change lives, they change the environment, and are very profitable for those who would like to participate in the sale of these products. Who would have thought people would come to see me on stage? Who would have ever thought I would be on a stage? Just a short time ago, if not for others who cared enough to share their enthusiasm for life and their belief in me, I would have never stepped on this stage—much less be basking in the glow of a successful presentation. To think...my life had consisted of painful shyness, often masked by irritating and aggressive behavior that had consistently stopped me from going forward with satisfaction and confidence. To some, the transformation seemed impossible—but they didn't know my secret weapon.

Even in those "shy days," my career was still considered successful by other people's standards, but their opinion of me *as a person* was mixed.

My work schedule was filled from five in the morning until late at night seven days per week. I was developing a pilot music program for over eight hundred children in the public school system (teaching their teachers), teaching in two colleges, teaching at the school of performing arts, being principle timpanist with a symphony orchestra, doing local musicals, and playing clubs on weekends, with an occasional jazz gig for variety. My mom used to say I was going in so many directions at once that if I died, they would never find all the pieces in time for the funeral.

It was out of control, and I really wanted to stop playing in clubs on weekends. So, with considerable fear, I started a MLM (multi-level marketing) business to try and accumulate an extra two hundred dollars a month to pay the bills. This very small dream forced me out of my comfort zone. These activities were exceptionally foreign and painful to me, due to my lack of experience and confidence. Yet today I stand on stage with my secret weapon! Amazing!

So how does a shy, gifted, introverted elementary school teacher, college instructor, and symphonic timpanist turn into a genuine extrovert; worldwide water, air, energy, and healthcare expert; and radio talk show host appearing on stage in front of thousands?

As with all major advances in life, it comes from the people you know, the books you read, the CDs you listen to, and the events you attend.

I had mentors who had introduced me to books, like *The Magic of Thinking Big*, that opened a new world of possibilities to me. They made me realize that I was my only obstacle to greater success and happiness. I had to make decisions, set markers for achievement, and accept temporary disappointment to move ahead. My immobilizing fear of failure was gradually replaced with little victories and successes as I took action.

Within months, I was out of the clubs and rapidly moving forward.

My first transformation came about because I took action on a belief in a dream that was greater than my fear of failure.

My mentors kept encouraging me to consistently "invest a little time and money into your personal development," and I devoured books and tapes from the greats. How to Win Friends and Influence People by Dale Carnegie had a huge impact. (I knew I still had a way to go when, after reading it several times, I was counseling with a business mentor who asked me if I had ever read the book. I answered, "Many times." His response: "Better read it again, Fred." Such was the level of my existing people skills.)

With the help of my mentors my business success was growing, but I suddenly hit a wall. My confidence was shaken and I
knew I was still missing something in my life.

Late one night I was counseling with my business advisor and
I experienced a life-changing revelation. The rest of my transformation occurred.

My mentor was a Christian and had tolerated many months of
my using the name of Jesus Christ rather inappropriately on a reg-
ular basis. His skillful patience was about to pay off. I asked Larry
what he was holding back from sharing with me. There was something missing in my life and in what I was doing. He looked at me
and said, "It is time."

Please understand, Larry had less than a high school education,
while I had a college degree and years of post-graduate studies, but
what he taught me that night was the secret weapon—he taught
me faith.

If faith is the belief in the unseen, then every personal or business success starts with faith. Every time you start to produce an
outcome in life you must have the faith it will come about, or you
will not walk down that road. When you take it to the next level
and develop faith in God, his never-ending love creates an amazing
outcome—the evaporation of fear. Fear of success, fear of failure,
and fear of fear itself simply disappears in the face of unconditional love.

Early that morning my life changed forever. Gone was the
emptiness in the pit of my stomach. It took many years to come to
this level of realization of God's magnificent promises.

So, as the applause dies down and I get ready to leave the stage,
I thank God for this incredible experience. I hold the secret
weapon in my heart, and as I turn toward the backstage curtain, I
know it is for *Him* that they truly applaud.

Fred Van Liew
Phone: (800) 659-4426
Email: fred@ewater.com
Web site: www.ewater.com/fred

C3 80 C3

Let's proceed to metanoia factor #3!

Metanioa Factor 3

Excuses are a precursor to failure.

Millions suffer from it. It's growing epidemically. The illness? Excusitis.

Signs and symptoms? Underachievement.

If you study underachievers, those who have never attained a higher lifestyle or ever experienced what the world truly has to offer, you will find lack in all areas of their lives, both personal and professional. You will additionally discover they have a book full of excuses of why they didn't, couldn't, and aren't.

They are people heading nowhere and of course—it's never their fault.

Once you understand that excuses are what keep you from having what you truly want from life, you have a choice to make.

You can choose to join the multitudes, who have as their prize possession a boat load of great excuses, or you can learn to identify, isolate, and eliminate your excuses and proceed with a life filled with achieving your ultimate objectives and desires.

The choice is yours. To have your desires you will have to "bust" your excuses and follow the proven path of people who achieve their dreams.

One of the first CDs we ever created is called *Excuse Busters*. This is a powerful CD for those who are tired of allowing daily obstacles to stand in their way and are ready to join the success crowd.

Successful people have common traits. In successful people you find:

- Fewer excuses and more planning
- Fewer excuses and more execution
- Fewer excuses and more confidence
- Fewer excuses and more fulfilled dreams
- Fewer excuses and more success

Successful people are often individuals who, in fact, had every right to make more excuses than the average Joe.

Countless individuals' success stories start with underprivileged backgrounds, while countless stories of failure follow those with the most resourceful and influential families.

As mentioned earlier, what distinguishes an individual who is successful from one who is not is clear and simple: it is their mindset.

Successful people allow nothing to stand in their way. Failures allow just about everything to stand in their way.

Successful people often turn what others would use as an excuse into their highest motivator.

"Too young? I'll show you!"

"No experience? I can find people who know how!"

"Poor health? I'll live till I die, let's go—move forward!"

Let's look at two of our successful coauthors and let their stories solidify these observations in our own minds.

Dr. Robert DaSilva certainly started out in a situation that would easily justify nonachievement..

DECIDE, VISUALIZE, EXPERIENCE

Dr. Robert DaSilva

The Charlie Brown classroom experience was my life. Sitting in first grade in Newark, New Jersey, I could hear the teacher and other kids speaking but had no clue as to what they were saying. Being born of Brazilian immigrants, I only knew Portuguese.

Within weeks, I was moved to another class. I could tell this class was different. The kids were not the same. These were the days prior to politically correct terminology. The class was dubbed the "retard class." I was totally humiliated before it was discovered that I needed help with English and was placed appropriately.

My parents were hard-working dedicated people. They never took sick days and would go long periods without a vacation. They would tell me, "If you don't work hard you will lose your job. People should always work harder than they are paid to do. This is what makes you indispensable."

My father was a construction worker for a foundation company and had to work in frigid weather. That was the only job he could get with a third-grade education. School was not important growing up. Just as on a farm, "hands" are the thing of value; with a family of thirteen, children were considered free labor.

On one of the coldest days in New Jersey history, the men were sitting in their cars staying warm. The owner of the company, Pete, came to the site to let everyone go home for the day. As he approached the work site, he found one guy hammering nails and constructing forms. It was my dad. He wasn't even wearing gloves, as that would slow him down.

Pete called out to my dad. He put his hand on my dad's shoulder and told him he wished he had a hundred men like him. That day he was warm, even though it was twenty degrees below zero. He was a man of no excuses. If there was a job to do, he didn't talk about getting it done, he took action.

My mother had a similar upbringing. Being the first female of eleven brothers and sisters, she was expected to help raise her siblings. She was only allowed to finish grade school. It was considered wasteful to pay for a girl's education, after all she would just get married.

Mom worked on an assembly line at Western Electric, better known by its modern name, AT&T. Her supervisor recognized her meticulous attention to detail and recommended her for a brand new department—data entry. It wasn't long before she was recognized for entering the greatest quantities of data with the lowest amount of errors. The company sent her to secretarial school and she honed her skills for a position assisting a low-level executive. Eventually that lower-level executive became the regional vice president of AT&T. He convinced her to postpone retirement several times. Ultimately, it took three assistants to replace my mother.

My parents are the living example of the work ethic. They always did more than expected. That rubbed off on me, so we were all greatly disappointed when I did not produce good grades in college. The distractions at Rutgers University made studying difficult. By the end of my sophomore year my relationship with my parents was strained.

I decided to take matters into my own hands and enlisted in the U.S. Marine Corps, without my parents' knowledge! On August 8, 1989, as I left the house to ship out, I placed a note in the mailbox telling them I was going into the marines. It was a bad move, but I knew if I had breathed a word of it to my parents, they would not have let me go.

In the recruiter's office they showed me a graduation video where some marines were in special uniforms, all decked out in white gloves and hats. He told me they were the "honor men." I asked how I could sign up for that. He just laughed and said, "You don't sign up for that. You get chosen if you are the strongest, fastest, loudest, and most disciplined in your class."

Those words echoed in my mind throughout training. Every night I visualized being the best of the best and graduating in that uniform. For the first time in my life, I had a goal. Every ounce of me wanted to achieve this lofty goal.

When I was chosen honor man of my platoon, I was astonished. I quickly learned this lesson: if you want something, you can declare it, make a plan, visualize it, and achieve it.

I had gotten "licked" by college, but I knew after my tour of duty with the marines was fulfilled, I wanted to return to school to become a chiropractor, and I wanted to graduate as valedictorian. I wanted to be the best doctor and help the most people.

After declaring this, I thought to myself: Who am I kidding? I almost failed college. But, my determination took me past those self doubts. I made plans and carved out a study schedule that I followed for three years as I attended school year-round.

I visualized myself on stage delivering the valedictorian speech. I would replay this scene so vividly that I could see my parents in the audience beaming with pride. I was so consumed with this goal that nothing else mattered. I knew I would not be happy until that day arrived.

It was a glorious day when I lived the picture I had visualized so many times. The real version was even better than I had imagined.

Years later I had the good fortune to attend a seminar taught by Dr. Ty Talcott on the subject of "radical forgiveness." I learned whatever you are *not* thankful for becomes a burden you carry.

If all the occurrences in your life help shape you and lead you on the path of your destiny, what is there to forgive? When that sinks in it is very freeing. It was easy to forgive my parents and myself.

My relationship with my parents is now phenomenal.

When you achieve a major goal, the feeling is wonderful but fleeting, like fifteen minutes of fame. What is more important is who you become on the journey and how happy you are along the way.

Dr. Rob DaSilva
Phone: (972) 436-4434
E-mail: DrRobert@painand injury.com

CB80CB

Declaring what you will have, sticking with it, and accepting no excuses is the key to being all you can be.

Our coauthor Rose Ruth is the example of avoiding excuses, staying the course, and accomplishing her dreams as well.

AND BABY MAKES THREE...OR FOUR...
OR FIVE...OR SIX

Rose and Leon Ruth

Sitting on the living room couch I could hear the rapid thump of feet running toward me. Soon I saw my child being chased by another of my children, as yet another approached from the opposite direction rounding the corner—very fast—on a collision course, just as everyone simultaneously spotted the two-year old and yelled, "Look out for the baby!" Bodies crashed amongst shouts and laughter.

Sitting there in shock it hit home: my family had nearly doubled in size—*overnight!*

Six months ago, at the age of twenty-seven, I had married my husband Leon, age thirty-eight. We were fully aware that we both had children: my two, ages two and five, and his two, ages eight and ten. However his children lived with their mother—until today.

What a change! It was great, but it was tough. All I could think was, what are we going to do?

I had always wanted to work at home, but the only way we could find to make ends meet was for both of us to work at "real" jobs.

All we had was what we made by working tough jobs and what the kids could manage to stuff in penny rolls while they sat in front of the TV.

I was not excited working as an office manager for dental and medical clinics, and to make matters worse, Leon's job as an electrical superintendent caused us to move several times in as many years. We lived in Prescott, Magnolia, Monticello, and Jonesboro, Arkansas; and Gautier, Mississippi.

This became tougher and tougher on the kids, and we finally decided to move to Memphis, where Leon's home office was located.

I was totally burned out. I still had a dream of working at home, but I took a job with the IRS. I worked my way up to senior lead customer service representative, and words can not express how much I hated it. Pure torture!

At what point does one give up? Should you just accept your lot in life? Absolutely not!

Maybe it took seventeen *more* years, but I finally met Dr. Scott Elliott and his beautiful wife Melissa.

What a change my life took. I caught his vision. Dr. Elliott owned a very successful company, Digital Consulting Strategies, and operated it from his home.

With his help, I learned about multiple streams of income, and with his assistance I was able to transition into working from home.

I loved the day I resigned from the IRS.

After that, I continued to learn about multiple streams of income from Dr. Ty Talcott and my involvement with his Inner Circle.

Today I enjoy the extra money we earn from our involvement in the many Inner Circle projects created by Dr. Elliott and Dr. Talcott. We have fun and create income with projects such as group real estate purchases, coauthoring opportunities, and product sales, to name a few.

When I am not working these projects, I function at home as the senior managing editor and professional recruiting agent for TrueScribe, a medical transcription company located in Arizona. I am truly living the life of multiple income streams.

When I wake up every morning I look out my window at the ducks and geese on our beautiful lake and count my blessings:

... all my grown children—Cody, who works for FedEx and on his degree in journalism; Michelle, a stay-at-home mom; Renee, an administrative assistant in a large law firm; and Mandy, who is an LPN working with handicapped individuals while she finishes her RN degree.

... my seven beautiful grandchildren, who I love and spoil until we are completely worn out (and then I send them home to Mom and Dad). What a true gift from God and a true joy in our lives.

... my husband, who lived through all this with me.

As I look out on the lake, I daydream of later that day when Leon, now retired, and I will do what we want when we want—fishing, cycling, paddle boating, or walking around the lake.

Did you give up on a dream?

On September 14 we celebrated our twenty-fifth wedding anniversary. It took a few years to get here, but the time would have passed if we had accepted our fate or if we went for our dream.

Never give up your dream!

Leon and Rose Ruth
Walls, MS
Phone: (662) 781-0966
E-mail: RoseRuth@midsouth.rr.com

CB EO CB

Some people give up their dream before they even start to accomplish it. They get their alibi or excuse in place before they start so it will be ready when they fail.

How much time do you spend creating alibis to save face? Is your alibi poor health, lack of education, lack of ability, lack of money, bad luck, or too young? (Here is the chronic progression of the "I'm too young" disease: "I can't start thinking about that now, no one will take me seriously." "Oh, it is too tough to start now; I didn't lay the foundation when I was younger." "Son of a gun, now I am too old!")

No alibis, no excuses, just full speed ahead!

Dr. Talcott's story clearly illustrates the power of busting through excuses:

> I clearly remember going into private practice at the age of twenty-one. I was focused on being a physician from the time I was sixteen and went to school year-round, nights, between sessions, and any way I could accumulate a needed credit. It wasn't so much that I was overly smart; I was immensely focused. Nothing took me from my path and I greatly accelerated the time it takes most people to accomplish this goal (many of whom, I am sure, possess higher intellectual skills).
>
> When I started my own practice I knew nothing about running an office, filing insurance, or compliance issues. I had to hire people who were older (everyone was older) and more experienced. That could have been intimidating and a perfect place to use the "I'm too young" excuse.
>
> It was scary. *Will they follow my lead? How can I control the situation?*
>
> But, I stepped ahead in faith and it was a wonderful experience.
>
> Some months later, the staff took me to lunch and said, "We had some reservations about hanging our future employment on such a young inexperienced doctor, but you were so clear on where you were going and so confident we could all get there together that we were excited about bringing our skills to your dream."

Wow, the ability to engage others in a dream, combined with the right attitude, attracts the right people. The result? Your power team: the team of individuals you surround yourself with in order to accomplish a goal to which you have committed. It is all about clearly communicating your vision and assembling the team to accomplish it.

 CʒℰↄCʒ

Our coauthor Garry Bills expertly illustrates the importance of clear communication and a solid team for living the life you love.

THE HOME TEAM

Garry and Andrea Bills

As with most couples, we have lots of friends, business contacts, and networks. One invaluable lesson we have learned is that no matter how many people we meet throughout our lifetime, one thing is most essential to our success: "We" are a team. We are our "Home Team."

Although we have separate careers, our ability to work together is essential in accomplishing our personal goals and ambitions.

Andrea, my wife, works in the area of business development. I, Garry, work in the area of communication processing and systems creation. These however are merely our vocations. We are much more than our individual careers.

Our ability to excel in our personal careers is contingent on our ability to effectively communicate with our Home Team. I have learned invaluable lessons through our Home Team, which have assisted me in every facet of life.

The most beneficial lesson I have learned is realizing that the only control I have over an individual is determined by my own ability to appropriately react and communicate about the situation at hand. The core of all business, the core of all life, is communication.

Effective communication can excite a crowd, sway major decisions, make or destroy relationships, or even mobilize a nation in a common cause. Andrea has always understood the vast power of clearly communicating in personal and profession-al life. I, on the other hand, was much slower in comprehending how communicating the right message at the right time can alter one's life.

Andrea started out as an office assistant for a visiting nurse organization in Austin, Texas, then relocated to Dallas, where she worked as an office manager for a physician in private prac-tice. Our need to ensure the highest form of communication between us began when we elected to partner with another cou-ple in business, owning a commercial wall covering distribution company. The success of this company relied not only on our ability to communicate effectively with one another, but now with two additional business partners.

It was tough economic times in the early 1980s. This did not deter us from the thrill, excitement, and potential financial rewards of being our own bosses. Andrea led the charge with this company, quickly creating the necessary contacts and contracts that resulted in a very successful business. Our partners elected to purchase our company outright. We were glad to sell and charge forward.

Andrea elected to utilize one of her contacts and secured a position with a large general contracting firm. Once again, her ability to communicate and develop mutually beneficial rela-tionships allowed her to work her way to the top and serve as assistant to the president of the company.

As years come and go, one thing always remains consistent: communication is the core to a successful life. Communication is required to open the door to new opportunities. Communication is required to develop the right team and ulti-mately bring each opportunity to a successful result.

Communication can even be brought to higher levels. Take my career for an example. I started in medical technology. When dealing in research, so much relies on your ability to ask the right question, then to locate the right people with answers to the question at hand. My ability, first to communicate with myself to formulate a logical question that if answered, would solve the current situation, then to further communicate with those around me to ultimately put all the pieces together, is often life-saving to patients depending on us to find needed answers for their particular conditions.

The realization that communication literally saves lives led me to choose communications as a full time career. I convinced a local "interconnect" company that was working with several hospitals and medical facilities that there was merit in having a detail-oriented individual on board with a medical background. I was quickly immersed in yet another essential form of communication: the ability for companies to coincide and link different specialties into one common project. I quickly moved on to larger and larger corporations, where I learned the entire spectrum of international business relations and the immense need for logistical and supply chain-related activities, inter- and intradepartmental software solutions, along with process evaluation.

Through our many years of career changes, we have come to the conclusion that friends, associates, business partners, employees, and employers are mainly looking for the same thing—clear and meaningful communication.

Andrea and I are at our best together because we have mastered the art of communication.

Garry and Andrea Bills
Phone: (927) 567-3393
E-mail: awbills@centurytel.net

C3&)CB

Are you trying to go it alone? Do you find yourself thinking, "I don't know how or what to do"? Try the power of the team, even when it is a team of two.

What other excuses are holding you back?

Here is a great excuse: "I'm too old."

Colonel Sanders was in his seventies when he founded Kentucky Fried Chicken. He died worth tens of millions of dollars.

We love the story of the sixty-year-old grandma who told her grandson she was going back to college to be a lawyer. He said, "Are you nuts? Five years from now when you graduate, you'll be sixty-five." To which she replied, "And how old will I be five years from now if I don't go back and graduate?"

Dr. Talcott's mother, Clarece (Misty) Talcott, is inspiring to all who know her age-related story.

A LONG TIME IN THE WILDERNESS

Clarece Talcott

Books and reading were my first obsession. As a child, I attended a rural one-room school where the only books available were textbooks and the Bible. While still attending fourth grade, I borrowed and read the literature, history, and geography books intended for the next three grades. I waited until sixth grade for the Bible—too many "thee"s and "thou"s.

It was in eighth grade composition class that I decided to be a writer. The assignment was to write a paragraph of description.

I spent the entire weekend writing and polishing that paragraph. Reading it to the class was to be my defining moment.

Monday, I marched to the front of the class full of confidence and expectation, delivered my masterpiece, and turned to the teacher.

Instead of the praise I had expected, she peered at me through her bifocals and demanded, "Where, young lady, did you copy that?"

She paid no attention to my denials and kept me standing there, humiliated and crying, in front of the class while she delivered a lecture on stealing and plagiarism.

I continued to write, but it was many years before I would allow anyone to read my cherished words. My favorite hiding place for my creations was under my mattress.

I finished college, taught school, got married, and raised a family, but I continued to long to write.

It was not until I was forty that I finally gave into my husband's gentle persuasion to enroll in a college creative writing class. Everyone was intrigued with my stories of farm life and the people, as I remembered them. The instructor pointed out that I was one of only a few writers who possessed the first-hand knowledge of a way of life that no longer existed, and its dialect. Only such a person could write convincing stories from that time period. He and my classmates convinced me I should preserve this knowledge in a novel. The story that I labeled "Neva" was born. Little did I know the distance between a novel's conception and its completion!

Shortly after I started the book, a well-known literary agent read and reviewed my book plan. She was impressed. Her words were, "You write it. I'll sell it."

For the best part of twenty years I labored on the saga of Neva and her turbulent journey as a Larkin woman, trapped in a family of helpless women surrounded by abusive and uncaring men.

Time after time I put the manuscript away, telling myself it was hopeless, but the agent's promise, the little writing group I worked with, and my determination to finish the story always brought me back.

When the book was finished (all fifty-two chapters and 857 pages), I called the agent. She was sharp and haughty. She told me she now had a full schedule of romance writers and did not want to be bothered with a new author and a lengthy mainstream novel. Whack!

Now began the search for an agent. Most publishers won't accept author-submitted manuscripts. After four years of submissions and agent rejections, the manuscript went back in the closet—failed, done, over with! My "long time in the wilderness," the book's eventual title, had been longer than Neva's struggle.

But I just couldn't stop thinking about my manuscript. I knew it was a great story for people who loved to read real literature (versus formula writing) and appreciated a true pageturner—and besides, I wanted to publish a book so badly. Then one day my son walked in, threw a bundle of stuff in my lap, and said, "It's time, Mom. We are going to publish that book. It is time to get on the Internet."

I'd never sat in front of a computer that was online. After debating with myself for a couple of weeks, I got my computer hooked up and hired a young man to show me how to turn it on. And I thought it was frustrating writing the book—that was nothing compared to the challenges that lay ahead. I gave up several times, but each time I came back determined to get the job done.

It was a long journey from eighth-grade humiliation to that unforgettable day, nearing my seventy-sixth birthday, when I first held my beautiful six-by-nine paperback in my hands. *A Long Time in the Wilderness* became a reality with my name on it.

I thank God for granting me the determination, patience, and perseverance to realize my dream, and I sure wish that eighth grade teacher was still around to see this.

Clarece (Misty) Talcott
Phone: (972) 722-5102
Book information:
Author: A Long Time In The Wilderness
Web site: www.iuniverse.com
Call: (877) 288-4737

ಉ೫ೞೞ

Age is never an issue. What is the alternative?

We have both personally changed our career paths several times.

Let's look at Dr. Talcott again.

As I was approaching fifty years old, I said to myself:

"I started being truly productive at about age twenty-two. I will probably be still going strong at seventy-five. I have accomplished more in the last twenty-six years than most do in a lifetime, and I still have twenty-seven years to go! Let's do it again and leave a larger mark on improving the world. Let's positively and meaningfully impact at least one million lives in the next twenty-seven years or sooner!

"No excuses!"

When you live your dream you wake every day knowing what you want, how you are going to achieve it, and how to create the self-motivation needed to accomplish your objectives.

This is truly the definition of happiness: knowing what you want and getting it. This produces joy and confidence. It makes you look and feel younger. It gives purpose and meaning to life.

Making excuses is *fatal!* It will rob you of life. It's time to eliminate "excusitis" once and for all.

We spoke earlier of the people who have their excuses and reasons in place before they even start something new.

We refer to this as the "Prepare for worst and hope for the best" syndrome.

Ever been around someone who says they are moving in a specific direction and have set out to accomplish a certain task, but their actions clearly demonstrate they don't believe they will ever get there? They are praying for rain, but did not bring their umbrella?

The second they are presented with an obstacle to accomplishing their goal, the "escape hatch" is utilized. The excuses are standing by, ready to spew forth, usually starting with, "I knew that would never work!"

Another statement we constantly hear is: "I don't want to think about that right now." This type of denial, or avoidance, allows outside forces to have control instead of you!

Preparation, for every situation, is critical to successful completion, so why would we prepare for the worst? Although hope is a positive emotion, it does not entail the needed planning and preparation to successfully accomplish the desired outcome. Remember: preparation is critical to every situation, while denial will get you nowhere in life! You will get what you are prepared for.

You must get rid of the "prepare for the worst" mindset. It will lead you nowhere.

Moving ahead is not always easy. It takes breaking out of your comfort zone—and that never feels good. Let's attack that with the next metanoia factor.

CB℘CB

On to metanoia factor #4!

METANOIA FACTOR 4

You are either giving up comfort for growth—or giving up growth for comfort

When you start thinking of taking action outside your comfort zone, instant fear is inevitable. This fear causes most people to stay where they feel safe and shuts down actions.

Think of your comfort zone as a large bubble that surrounds you. The air is slowly leaking out of the bubble and it is closing in on you. However, you can push on it from any direction and it expands and brings in more air.

If you push hard enough, it expands the bubble, but if you let the pressure off, the bubble closes in on you once again. Therefore, if you push you expand your comfort zone and expand your life potential. Don't push—and your world slowly but surely closes in around you. There is no standing still.

As an example, we know an advertising executive for a large multimillion-dollar corporation. This woman was immensely talented and had millions of dollars at her disposal to spend with the media partners of her choice. For this, and other reasons, everyone wanted to be around her. She was powerful and influential.

Then she chose to retire. She didn't realize that she had a comfort zone based on her position of authority and financial resources—both of which were instantly gone the second she retired. She immediately felt uncomfortable in social settings because she no longer had the ability to provide business to those around her. She was now just an ordinary person who, in her mind, had nothing to offer. She began turning down social invitations from her old friends and business associates. She didn't feel worthy of being in their presence.

At this point she had two choices that would inevitably affect the rest of her life:

Push the boundaries of her comfort zone and become comfortable once again in social settings.

Don't push her comfort zone and slowly fade away.

Unfortunately this talented, well-spoken, educated, successful woman chose to not push her comfort zone.

The result? She slowly lost her social skills and retreated to a lonely life of watching television from her couch.

What an incredible waste when you think of how simple it would have been for her to isolate her innermost feelings, examine them, and push her comfort zone to maximize the rest of her life after a very successful business career.

Are you starting to realize the critical impact that the way you deal with your comfort zone has on your life, and how detrimental it is to fail to expand it each and every day? Your life depends on it!

Once again, it is impossible to stand still. You are either growing or retracting. It is a tough battle because it is easy for your comfort zone to retract, but it takes great courage to expand it.

So, sometimes you just need to shake it up like our coauthor Ben L. Jones.

THE UNEASINESS OF IMPENDING SUCCESS

Ben L. Jones

"My name is Robert. I'm in marketing. What's your name?" he asked the comfortably dressed fellow sitting next to him on the plane.

It turned out the man next to him owned a small vineyard in California and was traveling to Texas to close on a distribution contract for his wines.

"It's going to be a particularly good year for the merlot," he glowingly shared.

This turned out to be fortuitous, since Robert was an appreciative connoisseur of the finer grapes and was in the habit of sending new exciting wines he discovered to his close friends and relatives. An order for several cases of wine made it a fruitful meeting for both.

This was what Robert told me when he first came to visit. It was his way of introducing himself to new and interesting people because, as he said, "You just never know who you are going to meet." How right he was!

Several weeks earlier I had visited Robert in California to look at a business opportunity that was the continuation of a journey that had begun many months earlier.

I was looking for a change. I had been experiencing an endless gnawing feeling that my world needed a dramatic makeover.

I had worked hard in my life and grown a successful check collection agency. This required building a team and working with thousands of clients, large and small, from all over the country. I felt I was making a difference in their worlds by offsetting losses incurred from those folks that liked to exchange less-than-worthy printed paper for worthwhile goods and services.

It had been exciting when we first spotted a little-known change in the banking regulations that allowed us to create a faster, more effective, and profitable business model. Initially, there was exhilarating energy in searching the answers to a thousand questions: "What are the best businesses for our services?" "How can we effectively communicate our story?" "How can we be the best?"

But after several years, something was missing. You know the feeling. You wake up in the morning and instead of energetically meeting all of the new challenges and opportunities you just sort of get up and do what you are supposed to do. You still do a great job out of habit, but inside "the voice" tells you...something is missing.

This was not the first time I felt that feeling, and I knew from experience that change was beckoning. So, I began looking, all the while knowing that, "When the student is ready, the teacher will arrive."

Eventually the teacher arrived.

I was invited to visit with a group of individuals who frequently meet to discuss and learn how to advance themselves both personally and in business.

The teacher that day was speaking on the topic of the 80/20 rule. You know the one: 20 percent of the people produce 80 percent of the results. But this time the presentation took a new twist, as it was applied to comfort zones. At first I wasn't certain this had anything to do with me. I was wrong!

The point was made that there was a comfort level for the 80 percent group, and there was a comfort level for the 20 percent group. "That makes sense. Everybody naturally wants to be comfortable," I said to myself.

"The difference," he said, "is what this 'comfort' means to the different groups."

Both the 80 percent group and the 20 percent group set out from their comfort levels and strive for impending success. Both groups experience the uneasiness of something new as they continue their task. The difference in the two groups, that which causes drastically different results, is that the 80 percent group interprets this uneasiness as being something "wrong." They immediately quit and return to their comfort level, thus never accomplishing anything of significance. Conversely, the 20 percent group interprets the same uneasiness as the exhilaration of new accomplishment, and they break free from their current comfort zone. The result? New levels of achievement, greater self-confidence, and an expanded comfort zone.

The 80 percent group never grows. The 20 percent group constantly grows. The difference? Their interpretation of the common uneasiness of new experiences! The exhilaration of new accomplishment propels the 20 percent group to new heights and levels of success!

My life suddenly made perfect sense to me. I was comfortable, and every time I experienced uneasiness I was immediately returning to my standard routine and comfort zone. Now that I understood the impact of my thought process and actions, I was eager to experience the thrill of new challenges and opportunities.

It reminded me of something I had written years earlier for my son when I wanted to impart some "wisdom of the ages":

You have to learn, in order to know.
You have to know, in order to do.
You have to do, in order to be.

After all, as Shakespeare had observed, "To be, or not to be, that is the question ...."

And I wanted to be!

With this new knowledge and understanding I was ready to push my comfort zone and meet Robert to discuss potential business opportunities. To my surprise, I was offered an executive position for an exciting organization whose purpose was to raise $100 million dollars for schools facing budget cuts. I would be working closely with PTAs and PTOs to raise money for critical educational programs, youth sports groups, and youth organizations.

Wow, this most definitely would push my comfort zone! How could I successfully accomplish such an enormous task? How many more candy bars or magazines could people possibly tolerate?

Oh, I badly wanted to fall back to the comfort of the 80 percent. The uneasiness felt like it was going to overwhelm me. Going back to my daily routine would feel so good right now. But what about a few weeks down the road when I, once again, realize that I am unhappy with this routine of limited accomplishment? I chose instead to embrace the uneasiness and accept the challenge!

As I drove down the road I thought to myself, *I need to take a different approach for raising capital.* I looked around at the hundreds of vehicles I could see and the light bulb went on-! Instead of children selling unneeded stuff like candy or magazines, what if we offered something the family could actually use? All families need to maintain their vehicles.

Instantly an entire new campaign for raising funds was born! Forget the $1 earned on things such as candy. With my new campaign the school could generate a whopping $20 to $40 from each family for something they actually needed and save money!

I contacted local auto service centers and explained they could participate in an advertising program that would direct local residents to use their service centers. The best part is there would be zero out-of-pocket expenses to the service centers. All they had to do was provide a discount on their standard services. Zero out-of-pocket expenses, zero risk, and lots of new customers? The auto service centers agreed without hesitation. Coupon books were printed to advertise special discount pricing for oil changes, tire rotations, etc., by the appropriate auto service center.

This new system is win-win! The schools generate needed income from the sale of coupon books. The parents and family members save money on needed services. The auto service centers gain new loyal customers with zero advertising cost or risk.

The program was a huge success and generated significant funds for the schools.

Mark Victor Hansen said it best, "Givers get."

You can't give all you have to offer when you are stuck in your comfort zone. I am excited about giving my time, my energy, my knowledge, and my "being."

I always embrace my uneasiness at the exhilaration of new accomplishment. Each and every day the 80 percent allow new exciting opportunities to pass them by, allowing the 20 percent to grow and expand.

In which group do you choose to be?

Ben L. Jones
817-715-4484
bjones01@sbcglobal.net

C8 80 C8

Like Nike says, "Just do it." Courage is not about going to war or jumping out of a plane. It is about taking action in spite of your fear, whatever the source of that fear. Your fear may be of conversations in social settings, relating your ideas to your boss, starting your own business, developing new friendships, or intimacy.

What is the source of your fear? What's holding you back from higher achievement? Identify it and annihilate it.

While you must step outside your comfort zone to grow, the majority of your current friends and family may not want that for you. You have to remember that they have a comfort zone, and you, exactly as you are, are part of that zone. If you grow, you threaten what is comfortable for them. Don't let this deter you from your own personal growth. Rest assured, as you expand your comfort zone and continually experience the growth process, new and exciting people will enter your life. New relationships will be formed. If you are married, include your spouse in your growth process. Include your children as well. If they understand the process and that you want to include them, they will typically help and often accelerate the process.

It all starts with deciding what you truly want from life and what is holding you back. You must break free and expand your comfort zone. As you start this process you will quickly isolate those who en-courage you and those who dis-courage you.

People who en-courage (or fill you with courage) help with the expansion process, while those who dis-courage (or take away your courage) hinder the process. These folks can strike relative to your business, personal, or health objectives. Often times, it is the difference of life or death whether you surround yourself with en-couragers or dis-couragers.

This point is perfectly illustrated by the courageous personal story of our coauthor Robbie Walker.

ENCOURAGE PEOPLE—SAVE LIVES

Robbie Walker

When you reach the rarefied air of a mountain's pinnacle, victory is defined by the depth of the valley left behind.

My husband died unexpectedly when I was forty-five years old, leaving behind a twelve-year-old daughter, Shannon, and massive debts. It takes an optimist to farm, always believing next year will pay off all the debts. When Shannon needed me the most, I was almost non-functional from shock and massive debts. We survived, but it took two years of working for minimum wages and a devastating bankruptcy. Bankruptcy is unequivocally demoralizing. I had to sell the land, something I was taught to never do. Answering the phone was a challenge, looking people in the eye, even a bigger challenge. My self-esteem and self-respect ceased to exist.

With Shannon's encouragement, I decided to go to college. After graduation I took a secure job and put aside the needed money for Shannon's education. She would become an electrical engineer. Life appeared to be on track and heading toward security and happiness.

I then found a lump in my breast. One of my worst fears was now a reality—cancer. Bankruptcy cannot even begin to compare to the total devastation, fear, and mind-numbing effects of that one word. Although chemotherapy saved my life, the emotional turmoil of the endless psychological and physiological effects was life-altering. I am surprised and thankful my daughter never left my side. To this day she remains my very best friend.

My faith in God, strong family ties, and loyal friends in many ways were more life-saving than the actual chemotherapy. I can never repay those who held my hand and kept my spirits high. You know who you are—thank you for saving my life.

After I learned I was in remission, I returned to Texas Tech and graduated with honors. Currently, I teach fifth-through eighth-grade mathematics in a small, lower socioeconomic school in Texas. Students are filled with insecurities, bad attitude, nervous energy, and lack of direction. With a new outlook on life, I was confident I could make a positive impact on their fragile minds.

It brightens my day and solidifies my purpose to see the look of astonishment on a student's face when a math concept suddenly makes sense. The student's confidence instantly increases, which aides in all areas of life, far exceeding mathematics.

It is no secret that educators are the poorest paid professionals. Many of us with families to support actually fall under federal poverty guidelines. The bureaucracy and paperwork is endless. "No Child Left Behind" places the entire responsibility on the educator and discards a student's inability or unwillingness to perform at expected standards. Educators are told to teach the students according to their personal ability and learning style, yet they are not provided the essential time and resources to make this feasible. These same students are then graded by a standard test with accelerated standards. Additionally, there is no funding available for up-to-date textbooks. Poor school districts are continuously forced to patch undeniable holes in our educational system while simultaneously attempting to effectively prepare students for their demanding future. These students are our future, not only here in Texas, but also in the United States and eventually the world.

Where is my purpose? Where is my reward?

I have always known that I would locate the people, resources, and relationships that would allow me to live the life I have always desired while allowing me to provide security and happiness to my family. I found this in the Inner Circle.

The Inner Circle provides an unparalleled professional environment for individuals from all backgrounds and careers to step past their current personal limitations and into an arena of personal development, wealth accumulation, and asset protection—all the while enjoying the rewards of life-enhancing new friendships.

Through the Inner Circle, I have realized the immense opportunities available to us all. A never-ending voice inside my head reminds me of the land I was forced to sell. Over the years I have been unable to purchase real estate. Now, due to Inner Circle connections and resources, I am once again able to own and profit from tangible land. Back to the top of the mountain!

I have also learned the immense power and necessity of goal-setting. I have taken this invaluable lesson and applied it with my students. It's amazing to witness what a child can do once their mind realizes it can be achieved. It's amazing what all of us can do once our mind realizes something can be achieved. Confidence is key. This is built one step at a time, always striving for the next level of accomplishment.

Each and every day I push my students to utilize their minds to think beyond the lines and paper. Life is abundant and exciting when you realize its possibilities. The Inner Circle has allowed me to see past my own limitations within our educational system.

The only one holding me back is me. The only one holding you back is you.

Expand your mind and horizons today. With each pentacle achieved, an even higher and more exciting mountain awaits!

Robbie Walker
Phone: (806)763-6237
E-mail: rjmwalker@aol.com

C3ED)C3

As you can see, confidence is built by an encourager.

A person is not necessarily a discourager just because they advise against an action. They may well suggest an alternative that they believe will better accomplish your goal, but someone who truly tries to take the wind out of your sails needs to be avoided if you want to rapidly make progress in your life. Encouragers move you out of your comfort zone by supporting the fact that you can.

Remember this inescapable power principle …

You are either giving up comfort for growth,
or
you are giving up growth for comfort.

Make an immediate plan to move forward. If you don't, your life will most certainly move backward.

On to metanoia factor #5!

METANOIA FACTOR 5

Catching takes place when you go where the fish are

Periodically, we have someone ask if we want to go fishin'. Our typical reply is, "Not really, but we would like to go catchin'."

You see it does not appeal to us to sit on a boat with a hook in the water.

If we want fish we will go to the market. After all, that's where the fish are. If we want the fun of pulling in fish, then we prefer to be catching. In other words, we will go if you know a "hot spot," where we are almost guaranteed to pull in lots of fish.

Most people spend their life fishing. They leave their hook in a little empty fish bowl and end up surprised when they never catch "the big one." How could they? There are no big ones where they chose to place their hook.

Their intentions may have been admirable. However, fishing where there are no big ones is as fruitless as wishing for success with no definitive plan in place.

Fishing is much like experiencing higher achievement. You must:

1) Decide what kind of fish you want. (What is it you are looking to achieve?)
2) Utilize the proper bait. (What skills, team members, and other assets do you require?)

3) Find where the fish are. (What product or service has an incredible upside? Where do you have a competitive edge? What books or people have the answer and know the market? Who has the deals?)

With this figured out, it's time to go catchin' instead of wasting your time fishing.

Our co-author Dr. John Boren is the perfect example of someone who decided to go "catchin'" from a bigger pond.

GO WHERE THE PATIENTS ARE

Dr. John Boren

I was standing outside the door listening to the music from within the house. I could hear loud voices and knew most of the folks had been "tipping back" a few already. I was about to walk in the door knowing I would have an experience I have had so many times in my professional life. I would walk over to a small group of strangers and introduce myself. Someone would ask "what do you do?" and I would say "I'm a chiropractor." At that point, someone would put their hand on their spine and say "Hey, can you 'crack' my back?"

I stood very still on the front porch as it struck me— that is what the public thinks chiropractic is—pushing on a back. It doesn't matter how much neuroanatomy I know and how the procedures I use affect the nervous system and help to normalize function of muscles and organs throughout the body. What the public knew was that I pushed on backs.

I know the mind only "sees" and stores information in the form of pictures, but that was the first time it became clear to me what "picture" was held by the general public relative to chiropractic. They see chiropractors as someone that "pushes" on backs.

I had to go back to the car and sit down for a minute. I could tell this thought process was heading to an important awareness.

How does the public "see" a surgeon? They "see" an image (probably from a show like ER) of an individual in scrubs with a scalpel in their hand.

How do they "see" a dentist? Probably an individual with a mask on and a high pitched whirring drill in their hand.

So how do people decide who they are going to seek for treatment? As a doctor I like to think it would be based on all the intellectual property available to make wise decisions about the most appropriate care for the condition. That night I realized the basic decision was actually made from the pictures held in their minds. In other words, they have a symptom and think, "do I need my tooth drilled, do I need something cut on, do I need my back 'popped,' do I need a prescription...?" and then they seek the type of doctor that matches the picture.

This was a major awareness as it simplified an issue with which I had been grappling. I had been trying to find a way to get out of the 7 percent box. Every year about 7 percent of Americans utilize chiropractic services. This means 93 percent do not think chiropractic is important for their health or it is not the correct procedure for their symptoms.

The question I had been asking was—how can I access some of the 93 percent that are not utilizing chiropractic? Now I had the start of an answer. The 93 percent did not feel that they needed their back "pushed"! This left two strong possibilities to get to the 93 percent.

Number One: better educate people on the benefits of chiropractic care. This is a noble purpose but, it has been done for a century by thousands of chiropractors and the same image still remains in the mind of most Americans. These efforts have increased the number of individuals who value chiropractic and created more people who understand the benefits of chiropractic but few have changed their "image."

Number Two: Use my doctor of chiropractic degree to treat people in unique ways.

I chose number two and my company, Lordex, was born. I quickly formalization protocols for the formation of the Lordex Spine Center.

Prior to my chiropractic education, I had designed and built exercise and rehab equipment. As a graduate of an engineering university (not as a PE) and as a chiropractor, I now had the background to develop a system to relieve difficult, non-responsive back and leg pain. I quickly transformed my image, and the image of my clinic, to a scientifically based procedure incorporating both Strength Restoration Therapy (SRT) and Lumbar Decompression Therapy (LDT).

There are now medical, chiropractic, and osteopathic physicians across the country using the equipment and scientific treatment protocols I designed for disc decompression. Even for individuals who have had multiple surgeries.

Things have come a long way from that evening on the porch. I am certainly glad I went on home that night—I figured there would be other parties but never a more important insight that would impact the lives of so many.

Dr John Boren
Lordex Spine Centers
Phone: 281-398-1700
Email: lordex@lordex.com

CR&&CR

He had choices. He needed a plan. He could have just sat around and "wished" for more patients. He could have found innovative ways to fight for his share of the market, but instead he decided to create a new market!

Most people are so lost wishing that they don't take the time to figure out what they are seeking. They simply float around aimlessly in their boats and hope a fish jumps in!

When they are asked what their coming year will be like, most say "Well, ask me in twelve months and I'll tell you how it was." They live day by day and see how it turns out. In rare cases, individuals actually start a plan, but they never take the time to acquire the right bait or to go where the fish are.

Having an objective with no plan is a wish, and wishing is like fishing without a hook. With any objective it is perfectly acceptable to have more than one plan. A backup or contingency plan is the best plan of all. If plan A fails to achieve the objective, then we will go to plan B, then C, etc. However, each one of these plans must focus on achieving the desired objective and not on what you will do if it doesn't work out. If you plan for the worst-case scenario, we guarantee this is what you will ultimately experience. Why? Because the second an obstacle arises you have already accepted the fact that it's okay to bail, and in fact know how to do it. This is the *escape hatch*. If you have one, you will almost always take it.

The reason is simple. Any objective that is "worth it" needs a plan. Anything complex enough to need a plan will probably take some work and hit some snags. When the snags are big enough and it seems too tough, you will tend to take the easier path, or the one within your comfort zone; therefore you will bail.

This reality is clearly depicted by our coauthor Stephen M. Giles.

AND THE BOATS BLAZED

Stephen M. Giles

I felt the sweat on my brow as I sat in the chair awaiting the verdict. At that moment I could not recall which great conqueror it was, but from some history class I remembered this story. He was standing at the top of a mountain with his men, awaiting battle, when they asked, "If the enemy is too strong, what is our plan of retreat?" In reply, he simply pointed behind him to the harbor where he had set their boats afire. I know just how they felt. I, too, had set my own boats afire. I knew the only way I would *have* to succeed was by placing myself in an all-or-nothing position. I knew if I left myself an escape route I would certainly take it.

It was July 2002 and my career as a regional sales manager of a large payment processing company was hanging in the balance. My straight commission sales force was a revolving door. As soon as I had a new rep functional, another would quit. I knew I had a great opportunity and I did not want to fail, but I had no more tricks up my sleeve.

The arrival of my director, David, at a team meeting was encouraging, until I realized he was there to demote me for lack of performance. I put on the best sales meeting I could. It was a very positive meeting for him to witness.

As stated, I had burned my boats and had to prevail, so I asked him the burning question, "What do I have to do to stay at this level?"

As I waited and the tension grew, I could see those boats blazing behind my head.

When David said, "One more chance, do or die," those were the sweetest words I can remember hearing.

I now had until the end of the month to turn things around. David outlined a series of exact steps to take. I seized the opportunity and set my course, knowing there was no escape route— no safety net. I was excited but not sure what to do. So I took my time and set up my own plan to support the path outlined by David.

I decided to create a plan and mindset that would not only excel in this set of circumstances, but would make fundamental changes in how I viewed and handled situations for the rest of my life.

I set out to make success a habit, maybe not always the easiest way or the fastest, but always the outcome.

Sure, you knew the story would have a happy ending. I met the goals set for me that month, and then David set out the next six months' goals. I met those as well, but the real story is how I changed to make success a habit.

First: always eliminate your escape routes. I learned if you plan what you will do if it doesn't work out, you will always take that path when the going gets tough. The amazing thing is how freeing it is when there is only one direction to go!

Second: I always spend the time needed to query those who have been down the path I want to travel. Success *leads* success. True leaders will always share their expertise. At a lower consciousness they will do so because of ego, and at higher consciousness they will do so because they realize you can have all you want in life if you are willing to help others get what they want. In this case, I reached out to other directors who were at the top of their game and then I duplicated what worked for them. I relearned how to interview, hire, and train, and ultimately how to lead, grow, and excel.

Third: embrace change and move out of your comfort zone. We all know that if you keep doing what you have always done, you will keep getting what you have always gotten, so you must do something new.

Fourth: surround yourself with like-minded, positive people. By hunting for, completely training, and holding accountable the "right stuff," our team finished fifth in the company that year, and they propelled me into the prestigious Chairman's Roundtable for top performers. By the next year my like-minded team finished third. I was not only back on the Roundtable, but also elected to the sales advisory council.

I had chosen this path and was successfully moving down it when I had the experience that serves as my inspiration to succeed in every aspect of my life.

I visited a friend in the hospital. Chuck was dealing with testicular, lymphatic, lung, and brain cancer. He was undergoing a vicious simultaneous series of chemotherapy and targeted radiation to his head and chest. Once 6-feet 5-inches and 240 pounds, he had now lost thirty pounds, all his hair, and the motor function of his right arm. Brutal stuff, painful days, and long scary nights alone in the hospital. Chuck was a decorated Marine and war hero.

After spending the afternoon with him, I left a humble and changed man. He was the most upbeat and positive person I had been around in years, and that was not the way he always was before his health challenges. He told me the reason was that he now had a focus, a mantra that was driving him. He said simply, "We have choices."

He continued, "I could think about all the negative and destructive surgery, drugs, and therapy. That is what most of the other folks talk about here in the hospital. But, I don't care about that. I choose to focus on standing in my dress uniform once again, carrying the U.S. flag at the opening ceremonies, dancing again, and swinging a tennis racket. I could choose to look back at the pain or *look forward* to the rewards."

I watched a man in a small, cold hospital room facing desperate odds look at me and say, "So many people have visited me, and I have talked to them about *choice*. I know they leave here and still *choose* their status quo, still live feeling desperate and afraid. I feel sorry for them. I pray that when I leave this hospital, I can go out and be a testimony to change."

To me, he has already been that testimony.

We all have choices. Most choose to see hard work and pain. I choose to see results and rewards.

I have my end in sight in the direction I am headed…burn the boats—who needs them!!

Stephen M. Giles
Sr. Regional Sales Director
Lynk Systems, Inc.
Phone: (469) 878-5965
Email: sgiles@saleslynk.net

C3∞C3

Who needs them indeed!

In fact, to measure if you are moving ahead with an objective, you can always monitor progress by asking, "How is it working?" If it's not working, it's time to make a new plan. It is not time to give up on your objective. So, anytime things are *not working* simply reanalyze the situation and make a superior plan.

Ask yourself: "Do I spend more time doing or getting?"

Most people spend so much time performing repetitious daily tasks that they don't take the necessary time to develop a definitive plan for achieving what they really want in life. The right plan with the right commitment leads to a life filled with rewarding accomplishments.

Our coauthor Kevin Roe shows us how making and sticking to a plan—even in the face of fear—pays off.

WHEN OPPORTUNITY KNOCKS, MAKE SURE YOU KNOW WHERE THE DOOR IS

Kevin Roe

Just a short while ago, I had dropped my son, Preston, off for his first day of school. He was so brave. He didn't cry, cling, hesitate, or even look back.

He had me beat. I was scared to death looking in the door of my new office.

With peripheral vision I could see the credit cards in my hands that had purchased the suite of office furniture, desks, phone systems, and accessories.

I thought back six months to the day my mind screamed out, "I quit, I quit, I quit! I am *NOT* a quitter but I quit!" That day in March of 1999, I had left my job with one of the largest residential property management companies in Dallas, Texas. That same day I became a stay-at-home dad, in our four-hundred-dollar-per-month rental property, while my wife supported our family of three. Bless her!

Our plan was for me to take six months and create "the" plan—both a life and a business plan.

I had been exposed to numerous jobs and had been moderately successful with several businesses—a software resale company, an auto body shop, and a candy company. In a word—*boring!*

At least I knew where I wanted to be and the source of my true passion—real estate. The only question was, "How do I get involved?"

Those six months were not only the greatest experience a father could have, but also produced a business plan that was exciting, posed unlimited opportunity, and created a laser focus for me. I knew my plan would outstrip the competition and I was excited to see how far I could take the concept. But right now, looking in that empty office, I could hear the voices of all those who said it was too risky. I hoped my belief was correct: "There is life after bankruptcy, but with no risk, there is no life." I further hoped I would experience the exciting life spurred by the successful outcome of a calculated risk, versus proving that life exists after bankruptcy!

The plan was to create Regent Realty company. The objective was to create a successful residential property management company that would set the foundation for other real estate opportunities. Regent was not created to play a volume or numbers game. It would not nickel-and-dime our clients at every opportunity—like most of the competition did. Success would be measured in relationships. Churning and burning clients ends relationships and necessitates constant new ones. Eventually the word gets around and you have no new folks.

Regent was to be the new face of property management. A company that gives clients and customers what they want. A company where communication, responsibility, ethical practices, being proactive, and giving more service than promised was the norm. Regent would be a hands-on company built on long-term relationships. Part of the plan was to minimize expenses with regard to repairs. Being hands-on and having personal rehab experience, I had an edge when dealing with contractors. I would even work on properties myself when needed. Pricing would be great. Regent would encourage, help, and influence wealth accumulation through real estate ownership.

This was the initial plan. I knew that if we could launch and accomplish this plan, additional people would materialize that would take us to other unexplored opportunities. It was to be an exciting leap of faith and a great ride!

So, take a deep breath, walk through the door—time to leap!

Wow! What a roller coaster ride to success.

Within just two years we were managing one hundred properties and the president of the Greater Dallas Association of Realtors asked me to chair the leasing and property management committee.

Personally, we moved into a larger house, we had another baby, and my wife became a stay-at-home mom.

We had arrived—we were established. The business supported our family needs, but I could feel the comfort zone closing in. Life could have just rocked along, but that was not in the plan.

Opportunity knocked. It was time to continue the journey. It was time to work less *in* the business and more *on* the business. It was time to develop a team and start letting go—time to delegate. I brought in an office worker who quickly became my assistant and an excellent property manager. As I learned the art of letting go, delegating, and the value of a team, I became freer. Now we could move to new heights. When the mind is free enough to think, magic happens. You can hire people to do tasks, but it is rare to find someone who will think for you and work *on* your business. It was time to create magic when...

... opportunity knocked. It was time to gain control over repair activities and costs. It was time to create my own maintenance company. I bought a van and tools, hired a full-time maintenance man, and DFW Turnkey Solutions was born. Soon, additional vehicles and maintenance people were needed. The guys of DFW Turnkey really showed their stuff when assigned a huge rehab that had been damaged by fire. Confidence in the ability of DFW Turnkey grew.

I love a plan that comes together! Property maintenance issues were handled more quickly and inexpensively than ever. DFW Turnkey was a success. My team was growing and then...

... opportunity knocked. I started bringing in more team members and formed partnerships with investors to buy properties that needed extensive work. After the fire rehab, the quality of our work was demonstrated at a new level. From that point forward I would buy a property, DFW Turnkey would do the rehab work, and Regent Realty would broker the sale of the completed property. Regent would then often manage the property I had originally purchased, rehabbed, and brokered at resale. What a great system to find, fix, sell, and manage properties— and I knew it was being done right at every step!

Then I started getting calls from investors and individuals who wanted to get involved in real estate but had insufficient cash, credit, or experience. I really wanted to help them get started. I considered putting a group together, but the time involved in maintaining group activity was prohibitive. The desire to help was there but the time wasn't. And then ...

... opportunity knocked. At that time, Dr. Ty Talcott, of Power Strategies Inc., had several personal rental properties under my management. We talked about our respective interests and he introduced me to his Inner Circle. What a match made in heaven.

He had an organization that wanted to get involved in real estate group purchases. Since the Inner Circle is based on the same philosophies, relationship and team-building approaches that I had had so much success utilizing, I immediately became a member. Dr. Talcott, his partner Dr. Elliott, and I started formalizing a plan to combine the desires of the Inner Circle with my complementary companies. DFW Power Properties was born.

DFW Power Properties hit the ground running with group purchases of rehab properties. Soon, many of the group evolved to owning their own individual properties and it continues to grow to this day.

I can't help but wonder what the next opportunity will be. Life sure is exciting when you can overcome your fears, build long-term relationships, and surround yourself with the right team. If you do, victory will be yours. Are you ready?

Kevin Roe
Phone: (469) 867-0447
E-mail: www.dfwpowerproperties.com

C3℘CℜC3

Preparation is a key that allows you to act when opportunity knocks and assists you in seeing "the next step" in life. Planning is the process of preparing.

It is absolutely amazing how many people continue to do what is clearly not working instead of taking the time to revise their approach in order to experience their desired results.

We all only have one chance on this planet—spend your time wisely and prepare every step of the way.

On to metanoia factor #6!

METANOIA FACTOR 6

People can't be failures

The only failure in life is the failure of a plan to accomplish an objective.

Once you understand that *you* can never be a failure, your self-esteem will skyrocket to new heights. People are not failures. The only failure in life is the failure of a plan to accomplish an objective. *You* cannot fail. Therefore, achieving success in life is as simple as closely monitoring a clearly defined plan and periodically altering that plan for the purpose of achieving your desired objective.

During one of our seminar events, a woman began to cry. We asked what was causing the tears, and she stated she had just had a major awareness that would dramatically affect her life.

She elaborated that for the last five years she had been telling anyone who would listen that she was a total failure. It turned out she had failed nursing school. During the seminar she began to re-evaluate her past and realized that it was not she who had failed. It was simply her plan that had failed.

At the time she had attempted to complete nursing school, she was newly married with a newborn child. Both her husband and child were demanding the majority of her time. Additionally, she was working forty hours per week and decided to go to school at night to become a nurse. *Bad plan!*

Her tears were actually tears of joy. Her husband now spends a significant amount of time on the road with his career, her child is in kindergarten, and she only works a part-time position. She realized now is the perfect time to go back to school and become a nurse. *Good plan!*

We are confident she will accomplish her goal with flying colors!

People do not like failure. The fear of failing, and thus being *labeled* a failure, is a major limiting factor for the majority of people.

Let's look at this example from Dr. Talcott:

> When I was about three years old, there was a child on television who did a summersault. My father asked me if I could do a summersault and I said, "Uh-huh." He replied, "Well, let's see."
>
> Instead, I acted shy and left the room. The reason was that I had never tried to do a summersault. So I went to my room and practiced some ugly summersaults until I nailed it. Then I came back and said, "Watch," and did a pretty good summersault.
>
> In this situation my fear of failure actually motivated me to practice in private until I had my "show" fine tuned; then I came out to show everyone.
>
> My dad was wise not to pressure me into attempting to do the summersault immediately. I was afraid to fail in front of him.
>
> What fear of failure is preventing you from taking action? Always remember, the only failure in life is the failure of a plan to reach the objective. In that case, you have two choices: change the plan or change the objective, and continue down your new path to a successful outcome. Never let the fear of failure prevent you from pushing forward.

෮෨෧෮

Our coauthor John Solleder illustrates this so well. Let's hear what a multimillionaire has to say about failure.

FROM HERO TO ZERO AND BACK AGAIN

John Solleder

As I sit on the porch of our villa overlooking the beautiful Pacific Ocean in Waikiki this morning, I am thinking, *How the heck did I arrive here?*

I guess in one sense the answer is "by airplane," but this is not the arrival to which I refer. How did I really get to this place in my life?

I think back to that fateful day, lying in the mud on a field in New Jersey. The hit to my back came from nowhere. I didn't see the guard as I was chasing the running back. Then pop, slam, dirt, mud, and the deep pain that ran up my right side. Then the operating room, the surgery, and six months of recovery. My dream of playing professional football was over; however, my ability to dream was not.

Looking back over my formative years, I had many things occur that lead me to think "outside the box." At age fourteen, I was already 5-feet, 11-inches inches tall and weighed in at 220 pounds. I molded my strength by training in my parents' basement for the purpose of playing football at the college level, with hopes of having a shot at the NFL. My freshman year went great. Co-captain of my freshman team and I was able to play several junior varsity and varsity games. During one of my sophomore-year games, I was chasing the ball carrier when I was struck in my back. Little did I know this split second would forever change my life. My body was instantly severely injured. I was hospitalized and learned I was born with a spinal condition call spondylolisthesis. Big word for a man who only wanted to play football, the game he had grown to love. The reality was that I would never play football again. My heart was broken, my spirit crushed. I went from "hero" to "zero" overnight.

The crowds of fans who cheered my name during every Saturday game forgot my name within months. It's amazing how fast one can fade into obscurity. My teammates, with whom I shared so much camaraderie, faded into the abyss. The coaches, who clearly communicated they were "always there if I needed anything," no longer had time for a washed up player and asked me to turn in my jersey. All my dreams of escaping the lower middle class and achieving what I thought was my life's purpose were no longer possible. How does one go on?

My dad, an electrician by trade, gave me a book by Dr. Norman Vincent Peale. Dr. Peale wrote about the power of positive thinking. Peale wrote, and these words are engrained in my mind to this day, "If you think you have problems, go to a funeral or nursing home and you'll figure out you don't. You have challenges. This means you are alive and well and therefore have the ability to take control of your life and correct any and all challenges!"

These words, to me, were as powerful as they were life-changing. I began to apply Dr. Peale's words to my life. After recovering from a spinal fusion and graft, I realized God had given me options beyond the gridiron.

A few years later I was speaking with one of my childhood friends who mentioned that his father had been offered millions of dollars for his company. He had created an oil additive that would extend mileage and protect engines. Several of the major automobile companies were interested in his work. Keep in mind, at the time I lived in a blue-collar New Jersey neighborhood. The fact that his father had a company was news to us all.

A few days later I saw his dad working on one of the many old cars in his driveway. I walked over and congratulated him and asked a question. "How did you do this?"

His answer sticks with me to this day. "I am an engineer by trade, but an inventor by passion. When all my well-meaning friends told me to quit and get a job in my industry I didn't listen. I told myself, *Frank, don't be afraid to fail.* After hundreds of inventions and patents, I finally achieved what I always believed I would. If there's one bit of advice I could give you as a young man [I was seventeen], it's: don't be afraid to fail."

This was my first motivational speech. Its impact on my life has been unparalleled.

I went home and started looking for everything I could read about business, self-employment, and self-development. A few short years later I involved myself with a direct selling company. I attended a lecture and heard Jim Rohn say, "For things to change you have to change. For things to get better, you have to get better."

I adopted Mr. Rohn's statement, have applied it, and shared it with hundreds of thousands of people. The rest is history.

I started believing that with God's grace and the right knowledge, anything was possible. I found the proper mentors with the information I needed. Finally, I implemented what I had learned into my own business. I earned my first million by age twenty-nine. Much more important than the money was the life experience. I have lived in, worked in, or visited forty-two countries. I've been blessed to attend the 1996 Olympics, several Super Bowls, and four World Series, and I've walked in the footsteps of history in places like Jerusalem, Petra, Cairo, and beyond. Today I have a lifestyle that a kid from the wrong side of the tracks could have never fathomed.

Well, almost time to fly again. Today we're flying over volcanoes. I am sure that will be amazing. I love volcanoes. They are the perfect metaphor for life. They have a burst of productive and eruptive energy, and they change the landscape around them.

In my case, what if I hadn't gotten hurt? What if losing what I thought was important had failed to bring me to a greater understanding of who I became in the process?

Well, part of a vacation is planning what's next. So it is in life. We presently have six separate businesses to operate. Each day brings new opportunity to grow and prosper. I rely on my experience and knowing that, although certain plans fail to achieve their objective, those who persevere will "fail their way to success."

John Solleder
Phone (972) 231-1122
Email: jsolleder@sbcglobal.net

CRSOCS

Remember you're not a loser if you don't win—you're only a loser if you stop playing.

On to metanoia factor #7.

The way to experience the lifestyle and benefits of the top 20 percent of society is to stop acting like the 80 percent!

Pareto's Principle is simple, straightforward, and proven: 20 percent of any given group do 80 percent of the work. Twenty percent of any given group also enjoy 80 percent of the reward.

It has been proven over and over that when you have a group of people doing tasks directed at achieving a specific objective 20 percent do 80 percent of the work. This rule is universal and applies to all areas of life. Twenty percent of people control 80 percent of the wealth. Twenty percent of people do 80 percent of good deeds in the world. Twenty percent of the population commits 80 percent of the crime, etc.

What differentiates the 20 percent of the population who possess 80 percent of the wealth, happiness, and fulfillment? Bottom line: it's the way they think!

Their perspective on life and mental foundation directs their actions. These actions produce superior results better than the majority 80 percent.

Understanding what *not* to do is more important than what *to do*! We are all born to thrive, but somehow during our upbringing we are programmed to avoid failure, to play it safe, to conform to what is expected. The result? Over 80 percent of individuals end up broke at the age of sixty-five, totally dependant of social security and family assistance!

Do you still want to conform? Do you still want to act and think like the 80 percent?

This poignant story by our coauthor C. Nolan Gray describes the traps of conformity to which he succumbed and the awakening that got him back on track.

AWAKENINGS

C. Nolan Gray DBO

Where have I gone? What ever happened to the real me? This was the thought to which I awakened. An epiphany, in a sense, that hit me like a ton of bricks. Somewhere between my inquisitive, risk-taking, loud, curious, athletic, fun-loving, outgoing, full-of-energy childhood and my self-conscience, apprehensive, withdrawn, sedentary, complacent, fearful adulthood, my drive, spirit, and authentic personality were lost. At that moment I decided I wanted *me* back again.

For many days I asked myself why I had allowed this to happen and continue for so long. Did this occur due to the fact that high-energy kids are constantly reprimanded, scolded, and told, "No. Stop that. Put that down. Be good. Sit down. Quiet down. Don't ask so many questions. Don't touch that"? Did this happen so many times by the age of twelve that I simply lost my will to express myself and discover the world? Had I, in the interest of being liked and loved, subconsciously suppressed my boisterous and effervescent self, in an effort to keep those around me happy and in approval of my temperament? Could this have led to the loss of my gung-ho and just-do-it attitude of childhood? That is the theory I have concocted thus far.

Several years prior, I had felt like a new driver on a touchy clutch—back and forth, back and forth. First, full-speed ahead, driven to succeed, and carry out my aspirations, then jam on the brakes, afraid to act upon those thoughts and desires. This produced a stalemate, caused by a vicious and endless cycle of personal and professional frustrations. One of these had to be eliminated to live with any sense of peace. Unfortunately, like most individuals, instead of conquering the fear, I simply chose to allow my desires and ambitions to fade and wither away.

When that realization hit, on a June evening, I began to fret feverishly over the plethora of missed opportunities I had squandered during that fifteen-year span. It was a somber experience when total comprehension of what I could have achieved, had I tackled life with the fullest of my abilities, hit me between the eyes. The more I thought, the bigger the possibilities became. What could I have become? Where could I have gone? What business success could I have enjoyed? What difference could I have made in the lives of others? What could my financial portfolio and freedom be like today?

After several months of dead-end contemplation and pondering, I found myself in front of the television watching the local nine. After numerous innings, and an equal amount of Guinness, I had the personal realization and acknowledgement that virtually all of the athletic stars in town were younger than me. Hello? How and when did that happen! At that moment, I began to hear a faint sound approaching from the distance. It was drawing closer and closer, and becoming louder and louder. But wait. It just couldn't be. I had heard of such encounters from grandparents, uncles, and other folks—mostly with gray hair. Why me? Why now? Tick ... tock ... tick ... tock ... tick ... tock. Oh no, it was that dreaded beast after all, nature's life clock! I couldn't really be hearing the life clock in my early thirties, could I? Yes, I could hear it loud and clear for the first time.

It turns out what initiated as a "nightmare on Elm Street" ultimately became the best thing that could have happened to me.

The fear of not maximizing my life and making a difference became far greater than the fear of stepping out toward accomplishment. The sudden realization that I was not immortal provided the catalyst I needed to seek the guidance necessary for success. I immediately shifted my precious energy away from dwelling on the lost years and on to the present, where I could accomplish with, provide for, and experience my remaining years.

Meandering aimlessly through life, like the masses, is a clear-cut path to unhappiness and mediocrity. I knew I needed education, direction, and time management. I found the best method to utilize my time more effectively was to stop doing unproductive activities and use that same time for high-payoff activities. The high-payoff activities I chose were simple, flexible, and inexpensive. I immersed myself in the New-Age Virtual University. This is a book and CD collection provided by the best-selling authors, corporate, and personal educators of our time. These resources can also fill your most unproductive time—in the car.

Once I began feeding my mind rich nutritious mental protein on a daily basis, everything seemed to change. My attitude, capabilities, awareness, willingness to risk, thought processes, and relationships improved dramatically.

Ultimately, it has been these personal and professional relationships that have made the most difference in my life. I know how important it is to surround myself with a team of individuals committed to success.

This transition has allowed me the opportunity to own several businesses and participate in proven, turn-key real estate investing through the Inner Circle.

How much do you have to offer the world? How much would you like to accomplish? How many years have you wasted "thinking about it"? Let me assure you of one thing—the clock is ticking. You better get started, as time is running out!

Stop thinking life away—start "doing" today!

C. Nolan Gray, DBO
Phone: (508)958-3042
Email: DBO@provenhealth.net

CBℰℭ

Are you noticing that our esteemed coauthors are having many of the same basic insights brought on by different life situations? We promise that the principles we teach are as much natural law as gravity, and by learning and applying them you can avoid many of these painful lessons.

Let's get you into the 20 percent as quickly as possible.

When you ask an 80 percent person what they do for a living, they answer in terms of their JOB (just over broke). Why do they have this job? To pay the bills. They have no superior vision of their purpose or direction in life.

When you ask a 20 percent person what they do for a living, they answer in terms of their career or profession. They have a purpose in life. They are continually growing and expanding their sphere of influence with other high-quality individuals. Their intention is continual growth and learning.

See the difference?

Eighty percent: job, work, sustain.

Twenty percent: career, learn, grow.

The 80 percent are never satisfied and go through life blaming others for what is 100 percent within their control. They never accept responsibility for the way their life turns out. There is always some person or other external factor that "caused" their circumstances.

The good news is that we are all born with upper 20 percent mentality. We were all born to thrive. The little baby does not drink milk to solely survive. The little baby drinks enough milk to grow and thrive.

Want to access the fast track to the upper 20 percent of society? Stop thinking and acting like the 80 percent! To accomplish this we must understand where 80 percent thinking is developed.

Eighty percent thinking is developed as we go through the trials and tribulations of life. Over the years we are programmed by society to play it safe and get a secure job. People waste their entire lives avoiding failures instead of planning future success. How can one ever logically think they will achieve a higher level of success when they trade hours for dollars and live paycheck to paycheck? This is, however, what society teaches us to do!

We are not stating that having a job is not needed or warranted. The following statement portrays our point with crystal clarity.

A living is made nine to five. A *life* is made after five!

Are you content living your life paycheck to paycheck? Or do you want to develop a *life* filled with accomplishment and fulfillment? Making an effort to become conscious of these destructive 80 percent thought processes is your first step to higher achievement. Once you begin to isolate self-limiting, destructive thought patterns, you will instantly begin thinking, acting, and achieving like the upper 20 percent!

To begin isolating 80 percent thinking, ask yourself the following questions:

Am I expecting my circumstances in life to change without establishing definitive objectives and a clearly defined plan? Do I expect things "out there" to change before I change the way I think and therefore the way I act? Am I accepting 100 percent responsibility for the outcome?

No objective? No higher achievement.
No plan? No higher achievement.
No responsibility? No higher achievement.

Stop stating:
"I wish it were different."
"It's their fault."
"How could this happen to me?"

To achieve higher levels of success you must regain control of your life by accepting 100 percent responsibility for all circumstances. Circumstances *do not* control your destiny!
You control your destiny!

Start thinking:

"I can do this."
"I will find a solution."
"I am going to do what it takes."
"Nothing will deter me from accomplishing my goal."

Power principle:
We live in the 80 percent and visit the 20 percent,
or
we live in the 20 percent and visit the 80 percent.

The choice is yours. The outcome of that decision is life-altering!

The *quality* of our thoughts is our consciousness. When things aren't going as you want, one question you immediately need to ask yourself is: "How would I evaluate the quality of my thinking on that issue?"

The top 20 percent don't allow circumstances to control their lives. The bottom 80 percent allow every circumstance to control their lives while making endless excuses. Their conscious mind is simply not aware of what is within their control.

Do you want to make positive changes or do you want to make excuses?

You wouldn't be taking the time to read this book if you didn't want to make positive changes. So let's raise our consciousness and begin understanding a critical component of success: your future is 100 percent within your control. Many times it may not appear to be, but you are the one who chooses how to react to situations you are faced with on a daily basis. These reactions lead to drastically different outcomes. Remember Dr. Talcott's duplex story. This situation could have easily been viewed as "out of his control." However, his reaction to that situation led to an incredibly different outcome. Think how devastating the outcome would have been had he just sat back and done nothing, feeling it was out of his control!

It's time to wake up everyone! Things may not always turn out as we anticipate or hope—but we are in control if we are conscious that how we *react* is everything!

You cannot change the conditions in your life without first changing your consciousness. Your situation as it stands today, including job, career, finances, debt, relationships, etc. is 100 percent a result of your thought process and level of consciousness. The only way to change your future is to change your mind! The definition of insanity is to do the same thing over and over the same way and expect a different result. What lies behind every action? A thought!

Therefore ...
Changing your thought process
changes your actions,
which changes your results!

This is 100 percent factual and proven.

We live in a society of instant gratification. Changing your thought process is an evolutionary process. This is why it is so important to feed your mind everyday with quality, educational, and motivational material. Remember, we were born to thrive—not just survive.

Our coauthor Mike Clements is an individual who started early on the path to thrive and proved our statement—we are born to thrive!

BORN TO THRIVE

I can remember, even as a small child, that I always had a burning desire to be someone special, to control my own destiny, to be my own man. I would always dream of being a football player or a rock star. The thought never entered my mind that those things were not possible. Of course, I had no idea of how to get

Mike Clements

there, but then again I was just a kid. I realize now that it's important for us to stay like small children in some respects. Three-year olds don't think they're too ugly or too stupid to be president of the United States. Anything is possible in a child's mind.

Do you ever hear children talking about growing up to be a mail clerk? They always look to the stars, "I want to be a sports hero, rock star, army general, etc." But as I grew older into my teenage years, I slowly lost the dream. Without a dream, I really had no direction and I ended up hanging out with whoever came along.

Fortunately, after years of struggling with the wrong crowd, I had the opportunity to join the U.S. Navy on January 5, 1978, and make a new start. The key is to get away from the people and environment that influence you in the wrong direction and cause you to take your eye off your dream.

I excelled in the navy electronics program. I studied karate, became a vegetarian (even though I hate vegetables), and started reading the Bible. What a change, but I loved it. My stint in the navy was enjoyable, but did not further me in regard to my search to be someone special. So, after four years, I left. I realized there was something else out there for me. I had no idea what, but I was about to find out.

I went to work for a defense contractor in Dallas, Texas, utilizing the electronic skills I learned while in the navy. This provided me a safe job in August of 1982. My goal was to get a couple of years experience while working on my bachelor's, then master's degree, in electrical engineering.

However, the following month I made a friend in the shipping and receiving department, and we started talking about music. Music has always been a huge part of my life. I started tinkering with the guitar when I was sixteen. I told him I played a little guitar and he told me that he wrote lyrics and sang. We eventually decided to get together and play a little. It was wild! We had immediate chemistry. I would pick out something on the guitar and he would add lyrics.

I never had the intention of starting a band, but our chemistry was so good we decided to start writing together. When we started writing, I started dreaming again. The next thing I knew, we were looking for a bass player and a drummer and making a run at getting a record deal. Talk about a leap of faith! I had a dream and really didn't consider the fact that we could fail. There was that burning desire to be someone and do something special with my life. Wow, what a great feeling that was.

In 1984 we found the bass player and drummer we were looking for and formed a band called 4 Reasons Unknown. In 1986 we were signed to Epic records with CBS and were the opening band for such greats as Miami Sound Machine, Mister Mister, The Romantics, and The Fabulous Thunderbirds, to name a few. We produced an album and several music videos, two of which saw some decent rotation on MTV. We reached a level that most people never aspire to, and most importantly, we got a chance to follow our dream. After years of living the dream, we broke up in 1989 and moved on with our lives. It was one heck of a ride and I will always treasure those moments.

After the band, it was tough making the transition to a new reality and move on. It had to happen. I got married to the girl I'd been dating since 1981 and moved on with my life. I decided to build on my navy and electronics background and started sending out résumés. I was eventually hired by a computer company in

1989 to build a services department for the installation and maintenance of computer systems.

I became an executive at that company and gained an enormous amount of business experience. However, there was still something missing. I had a desire to have control of my own destiny and be my own man. So, in 1992, while still employed at the computer company, I started a business on the side. I thought if I could get it going part-time, I could eventually go full-time and make a go of it. What happens when you live your dream and it's over? You get a new dream!

In 1994 I did just that. I quit my job and went full-time with my new venture. What I didn't realize is how hard it is to go it alone in business. I certainly had my share of scrapes and bumps along the way but was able to make it work. Here I was quitting another secure job, going outside my comfort zone, and giving up comfort for growth, but you have to take the leap if you want to be somebody.

Currently I am vice president and part owner of a software company in Dallas, Texas, called Diem Technologies. We are a leading provider of business information delivery solutions that help businesses small and large automate the delivery of messages, data, and documents. I now have the freedom and independence that I have been longing for.

No, you're not going to see me on the cover of *Rolling Stone*, but relative to that burning desire to be someone special, to control my own destiny, to be my own man—this I have achieved!

Two people look out the same window each night. One sees the mud the other sees the stars.

Mike Clements
Phone: (972) 669-3700
Email: Mclements@diem.com

CRENES

Da Vinci's *David* is considered to be the most perfect statue ever sculpted. When Da Vinci was asked how he created such a perfect statue out of a piece of marble he said, "I did not create the *David* out of stone. *David* was always in the stone. I simply removed everything that was not him."

We are all born to thrive. We are all born in the top 20 percent. Along the way we get plagued with society's negativity, mediocrity, and cynicism. We take on this baggage and add layer after layer on our shoulders until we are barely recognizable. To once again be in the 20 percent, you simply remove all that is not you and let your thriving nature shine through.

Our Inner Circle member and coauthor Charlie Cregor shows the importance of faith in your own ability and leaving behind 80 percent thinking.

ECONOMIC MUSICAL CHAIRS—ODD MAN OUT

When you look up and see the underside of "bottom" you know you can't go lower.

By the fall of 2003 I was looking up at the underside of bottom. I was the victim.

In the game of economic musical chairs, when the music stopped, I was left standing.

Charlie Cregor

I was totally burned out on my real estate career. Everything had conspired to destroy me. It all started with the presidential election of 2000. It took thirty-six days to unravel who our next president would be and it went downhill from there. The stock market crashed in the spring of 2001, and the telecom bust cleared out large corridors of rental real estate in the Dallas area. This was combined with huge corporate scandals and of course the tragedy of 9/11. To top it off, I then experienced three major contracts that went bad, including one property in which an alcoholic seller had stopped making his mortgage payments for a period of six months while I was marketing his property—and then it turned up with black mold! There went a three-hundred-thousand-dollar sale!

The glory days of the late 1990s in residential real estate were dead and gone to me. My immediate knee-jerk reaction was to consider a "real" job. Nine-to-five and a paycheck, but I decided to first try some of the many network marketing programs available. I guess I didn't realize you can't get something for nothing and to be successful in networking you have to work and be involved with a stable company that has a marketable service or product. I chose poorly, and the failure simply put one more nail in my mental coffin.

I then decided to revert to my college days. I started drinking like a frat boy. I soon found that a forty-one-year-old body does not recover at the rate of a teenager!

If I didn't make some changes in my lifestyle it would surely kill me.

I was at the bottom and on the way out for good when the best possible thing happened. Due to my involvement with a networking company, I had the opportunity to attend a training conducted by Power Strategies Inc. entitled "Power Strategies for Life Prosperity." Dr. Talcott and Dr. Elliott were training people from the networking group, along with other individuals, on principles and techniques that are used to get what you want out of life.

Their training unleashed my human potential. I quickly realized I was playing the victim and in that role I had no power. As long as someone was "doing it to me" I had no way to alter the situation. I saw my life as a game of economic musical chairs where *I* was left standing but *others* still had a seat! There were still houses being sold, but someone else was selling them. Others were making sales and building relationships to gain market share and loyalty. They were making a living through the tougher times and positioning for the big dollars when the market once again returned.

I decided "no more victim!" I embraced their teaching of the 80/20 rule. If 20 percent of the people have 80 percent of the wealth and success in the world, I want to be part of the 20! I decided to become part of the 20 percent and never tolerate mediocrity again. I studied and learned the thought processes and actions taken by the 80 percent and moved those out of my life to allow the natural process of thriving to shine through.

I had many blocks and fears during the turnaround, but I was confident that with the help of a Power Strategies exercise called Turning Fear into Faith and Confidence, I could achieve what I truly desired from life.

Over a nine-month period I consistently utilized the methods and techniques I had been taught. I implemented dozens of changes in my actions and thought processes. I was moving along this path and became supercharged from an incredible exercise we performed at an Inner Circle meeting. We brainstormed, as a group, how we would form a twenty-million-dollar net profit company. It changed my life once again! I now believe there is an excellent chance we will create one or more very profitable companies, and it made me revaluate my goals in real estate as well.

By changing my brokerage firm and revising my goals, I am back on top of my game. I am exactly where I should be—helping people find the home they want for their piece of the American dream. I am back on purpose, utilizing the skills I have honed over the past twelve years. My goal is to honestly and ethically close two million dollars of property over the next three months. I have no doubt my new approach, coupled with the ongoing teachings of the Inner Circle, will accomplish this goal!

What a blessing it is to be happy once again!

Charlie Cregor
Phone: (214) 417-6427
E-mail: ccregor@sbcglobal.net

CRCRCR

It's time to act like Charlie and stop thinking like the 80 percent. Break free from underachievement. It's time to raise consciousness in order to truly thrive. *Are you ready?*

Bring on metanoia factor #8!

METANOIA FACTOR 8

The motivation is in the objective

We constantly have people ask us to help motivate them. We cannot motivate others, only you can motivate yourself.

What most fail to realize is that the motivation is in the objective. If you are on a path that is right for you, then you wake up ready to go! How much does someone have to motivate you to play your favorite game? Not at all! When you set out to play (the objective), the motivation is inherent in it.

Turn work to play and there is no more work to be done.

This is best accomplished by finding your "magnificent obsession."

When you identify your purpose, what gets you fired up every day, you have found your magnificent obsession. If you are having trouble finding it, this may help. Fill in the blank. "If I died tomorrow it would have all been a waste because I never got to _____."

If something jumps in that blank, you better pay attention. You just said your life would be a waste if you didn't do, see, or accomplish whatever it is.

Pay attention to it. It may be something far-fetched that you have to creatively alter to pursue. Or something impossible that will necessitate looking deeper at what *need* it fills and then coming up with something different to fill the need. You can also have someone ask you the question periodically, as it is okay to have more than one answer.

Our coauthor Dr. Terry Yoder always knew his magnificent obsession.

PARADISE LOST, PARADISE FOUND, PARADISE WITHIN

Dr. Terry Yoder

Work, work, work! To a teenage boy on a Missouri farm, chores are a way of life.

Where had paradise gone?

Like all my friends at that age, I wanted to be a bodybuilder, but farm work was not the way to accomplish it.

I can clearly remember sitting in a pasture on a beautiful Missouri day and thinking about paradise lost. That day I could clearly remember the medical kit my parents gave me at age six. It included a microscope, stethoscope, and medical tools for my healthcare practice.

Even at the age of six I knew my magnificent obsession, and in fact my destiny, was to help others. I even remember walking and talking with my God on a daily basis. In many of those conversations I was seeking the answer to the age-old question: "Why are we here?" Heavy questions for a small child, but somehow even then I knew that if you don't know your purpose you have no reason to get out of bed.

I was born in Sarasota, Florida—the "sunshine state" and pure paradise. One day my dad came in my room and started telling me about an exciting change we were going to undertake. We were going to be able to feed baby calves and chickens and ride our horses in pastures bigger than the golf course we presently lived on. I was so excited. Many of our well-meaning friends and family were asking us why we would move to "misery." I loved my dad's response: "So what makes you think it is all roses here?"

Whether it turned into our new poison or passion, at the age of eleven, we moved to our new farm in Missouri.

What a magical summer that was. It was like a six-month camping trip. We lived in a two-room shack where you had to heat water on the stove for a bath, as there was no plumbing. We had to live this way for several months until our new house was built.

Way out on a farm you would think loneliness would be a problem. No way! I was far from lonely because most of my Florida friends came to visit. They loved running over two hundred acres of land and sleeping in the barn! What a dream for a Florida kid!

That fall, the start of the new school year was a real shock. What a culture change. My best friend, Mark, accurately described me as being "green" when I asked why kids weren't getting kicked out of school for swearing like sailors. I had never heard kids use that kind of language.

Despite my many challenges and adaptations, one thing never changed—my passion for nurturing farm animals. We soon had cows and calves, hundreds of chickens, pigs, two horses— Red and Beauty—and a new puppy from the sale barn where the livestock were bought and sold. Pure paradise!

Then the "work, work, work" teenage years hit. Where had paradise gone? I knew my attitude had changed and I had lost touch with my passion.

Luckily, those years of physical effort created a belief that hard work is what success is made of. I found a satisfaction in this knowledge, and it brought me back to my destiny of helping others.

I continued with great physical effort through high school and even worked extra hours in the farrowing house with newborn pigs on a 115-hog farm.

It was logical in my mind that I would pursue becoming a veterinarian. That is until I actually started working with a vet. I soon discovered the life of a veterinarian was not for me. I needed to help *people*!

I had always loved the natural healing capabilities of chiropractic care. Universal intelligence is what had led my journey thus far. This same universal intelligence also encapsulated the spirit of healing for all mankind. I chose to follow my instincts and passion and soon found myself accepted into Cleveland Chiropractic College in Kansas City. I instantly knew I had finally found my magnificent obsession to help people through natural healing. What an incredible feeling to know your life is being led by something you truly love to do.

Just before graduating in April 1986 I met and married my lovely bride Lisa. Armed with my doctorate degree and a supportive wonderful wife, I was ready to heal the world. I began active practice by assisting a very successful doctor who taught me the business side of healthcare. Within one year I stepped out into my own practice. I now had my wife and a newborn to support, so it was time for me set some "real" goals. I set a goal to have one thousand patient visits from August 1, 1987 to December 31, 1987. I was greatly pleased when we far surpassed this goal with 1,500 patient visits. I was on my way to my own successful practice!

My passion to educate patients on healthy living habits was stronger than ever. My very first healthcare mentor taught me the following invaluable lesson:

"Life is a journey in search of what we have always had but failed to recognize—the ability to both give and receive unconditional love."

Powerful! The daily interaction with my patients was mutually fulfilling, however, I desired a higher form of interaction. I began working with a nutraceutical (naturally occurring food supplement) company that functioned on a network marketing platform, which allowed me to interact and develop business relationships with individuals from all backgrounds, careers, and professions—all of whom were serious about achieving more in life! What an incredible opportunity!

Through this venture we additionally were able to work with the world leader in personal development, Nightingale Conant Corporation. Its speaking and leadership training was invaluable.

Each step in your life leads to the next. You simply need to recognize the opportunities along the way and capitalize on them as they are presented to you. I longed to develop close relationships with the very best. Those 100 percent dedicated to achieving the ultimate health, wealth, and happiness. I found this in the Inner Circle. How rewarding and beneficial to belong to an elite group of high-quality professionals all dedicated to assisting each other in taking their lives to the next level of personal and professional prosperity.

My continued passion of assisting others in creating their own passion and paradise provides unparalleled excitement and fulfillment. Its foundation being unconditional love, rewarding friendships, and hard work, all while remaining open to new opportunities that refine my personal passion. My paradise within!

Dr. Terry Yoder
Phone: (816) 223-7640
Email: www.ParadiseDevelopers.net
www.doctorparadise.com

CREDCR

Find your magnificent obsession and every day will be filled with energetic pursuit.

On to metanioa factor #9.

METANOIA FACTOR 9

Mistakes and failures are the building blocks for success

There are certain prerequisites for success—none of them have to do with being "right." People spend their entire lives being "safe" so they can never be viewed as being "wrong." Who cares if you're wrong! It's better to be wrong than to be safe as long as you learn from your mistakes. Instead of worrying about the mistakes you may or may not make, awake each day with confidence, knowing that all decisions and actions are only as good as the information available to you at the time. As you become more conscious, you will learn that mistakes are in fact the basis of all learning.

Making mistakes and making repetitive mistakes are two completely different matters. To grow and evolve you must learn and improve on a daily basis. Never allow yourself to continue making the same mistake over and over again. In fact, once you have made a certain mistake, never allow yourself to make this same mistake again.

As you diversify into new areas of life you will inevitably experience new mistakes. This is normal, acceptable, and the only way to truly grow, mature, and develop needed experience. The reality is each of us has specialized knowledge in different areas of life. As an example, you probably have a certain hobby that you enjoy. We guarantee that your knowledge in this arena far exceeds our knowledge. If we were to seriously undertake that hobby we would make tons of mistakes. How long did it take you to learn to ski or to ride a bike?

How do we turn knowledge into life advancement? Are you in a particular job or career you feel has limited potential? Do you feel you are not able to advance due to confinements of daily life? What will change that?

Let's look at the prerequisites of success and how you can apply these proven principles to skyrocket your personal success regardless of your current situation.

Success prerequisites: Willingness. Faith. Focus. Practice.

Are you truly willing to do what it takes to achieve your ultimate objectives and dreams? Or are you like the multitudes who wish for things to happen. Wishing will get you nowhere in life. If you want to achieve more, the process must start in your mind. Without controlling your thought process you are guaranteed mediocrity at best.

You must "up-level" yourself from the category of "conditional willingness," meaning "I'll do it if it is not too hard or doesn't take too much time," to the functional level of "unconditional willingness," meaning "I will do whatever it takes to get it done!"

Take a look at this tale of unconditional willingness and courage by our coauthor Dr. Billye Hansen.

THE MOUNTAIN IS IN YOUR MIND

Dr. Billye Hansen

"How can I peddle a bicycle 2,500 miles when I haven't ridden since third grade?" I said to my husband as I was reading the letter I held in my hands.

"I think that would be great. I've always wanted to peddle cross-country. What have you got there?" he asked.

What I had was a letter from Epsilon Sigma Alpha (ESA), a women's service organization that was desperately looking for an ESA couple to ride a tandem bicycle from Memphis to Los Angeles to raise money for our international fundraising project—St. Jude Children's Research Hospital. The original couple had backed out at the last minute.

My husband's enthusiastic response elicited a "You've got to be kidding?!" from me, but since he was forty-one and I was eighteen years younger, I surely didn't want to be shown up, so I meekly said, "Well, I guess we could volunteer."

The next month was a whirlwind. We arranged living quarters for our two young boys, we rented our house out for the summer, and we completed our job responsibilities. Needless to say, there was no time to practice riding a bicycle, and neither one of us were exercise enthusiasts. As the deadline approached I kept praying for a miracle!

My mother's words, "You can do anything you make up your mind to do," kept ringing in my ears. I hoped she was right!

We arrived in Memphis to a great fanfare. We were greeted by Danny Thomas, founder of the hospital, and all the gracious staff. After our tour of the hospital, we were even more determined to tell the world about this wonderful facility and the lives that were being saved.

The next day my husband and I waved good-bye to the throngs gathered for our send-off. There were many of my ESA sisters, along with Danny Thomas, the doctors, and patients waving back on that bright May day.

As we peddled across the Mississippi River toward Los Angeles I had never felt so alone, and there were 2,500 miles staring us in the face.

One of my husband's students drove ahead of us in a donated truck carrying an extra bicycle, spokes, water, and snacks. He would drive five miles, wait for us to peddle up, and take off again. We weren't totally alone—it just felt that way.

At least we didn't have to plan the trip. ESA headquarters had our sixty-three-day route mapped out and arranged to have motel rooms and meals donated—all we had to do was peddle!

Luckily, the terrain in eastern Arkansas is flat rice country, so the first few thirty-mile days weren't so bad. We actually enjoyed the peaceful countryside and the quietness of this environment. Our eighteen-speed French-made tandem made the going much easier than it would have been had we been stuck on the old heavy Schwinn bike I had grown up with as a child. I began to believe I might accomplish this cross-country goal.

By the time we reached Arizona, we were peddling one hundred miles per day. It was July and the heat was unbearable. We would get up around three in the morning and finish our day by noon to avoid being scorched.

Then came the trek from Show Low to Globe. This was ninety miles of treacherous hairpin curves through the Salt River Canyon; but worse than that, there was nowhere to stop along the way—we had to peddle all the way through and out the other side! We dropped it in low gear and peddled, peddled, peddled, while seemingly going nowhere. Every time we came over a rise I would think we were starting to head downhill toward Globe, but instead we'd face another mountain.

We had been on the bike thirteen hours in 104-degree heat. We had consumed six gallons of water and we were facing another huge mountain—I couldn't go on. Exhaustion forced me off my bike. I sat down on one of those hairpin turns and started crying. Soon my husband sat next to me and we began to talk about the patients at St. Jude Children's Research Hospital and how they'd have to sit bravely for hours with drips in their little arms. Once again, St. Jude became an inspiration. My physical pain and self-pity disappeared. If they could endure that, I could surely conquer the mountain in front of me!

We got back on the bike and took on that mountain. Our reward? A sign at the top that read: Downhill Next 8 Miles.

I was so fortunate to have this life-changing experience early in life. It has served me well over the years, especially in relationship marketing.

In that industry I have experienced many broken appointments, disappointing business relationships, and even companies that have gone out of business, but I kept peddling up the mountain until I found the right company to make my dreams come true—it led me to the sign that says "Welcome to the top!"

What a valuable lesson I learned on that hairpin turn that day. The mountain is in your mind. Change your perspective, ramp up your belief and confidence, and you are no longer controlled by the mountain—make it to the top and you will find that in actuality, the mountain has raised you to new heights.

Dr. Billye Hansen
Phone: (405) 341-5695
Email: www.yourmavad.com

C3&CR

To go to the top you must advance from "doing what you are will-ing to do" to "being willing to do whatever it takes." Can you see the difference? Success isn't easy. If it was, everyone would be suc-cessful! Success, however, isn't hard either. It simply takes under-standing and applying these proven principles.

Our actions are always a result of our thought processes. For instance, if your mind is unclear of whether a situation will work out as you desire, your actions will reflect this uncertainty and lead toward failure. On the other hand, if you are unconditionally focused on achieving a successful outcome, you will overcome all obstacles that stand in the path of meeting your objective.

Our coauthor Denny Lane and his sister Debra Lane Wright have a wonderful tale of willingness, faith, and focus.

PLANTING SEEDS—WITH PURPOSE

Denny Lane and his sister Debra Lane Wright

We are brother and sister baby boomers. Our parents are aging. They appeared to be liv-ing the good life in their Midwestern town. The family owned hardware store was a fixture that for nearly one hun-dred years sustained them, despite the arrival of Wal-Mart and Home Depot. To outside observers, their circumstances appeared stable and comfortable. It took a minor medical issue to reveal the true picture.

It was a minor burn that didn't heal properly and turned into an extended hospital stay for Dad. Being a sole proprietor, his absence was critical, so we volunteered to help out. We were not prepared for what we discovered!

The business was toast; medical insurance was about to ter-minate and life insurance was nonexistent. Contributing to the circumstances, the doctors suspected that Dad suffered from

Asperger's Syndrome. It was obvious that they needed help. But who could do it?

It was clear that it was us or no one. We soon found that the magnitude of the problems paled in contrast to the lack of creative solutions from advisors. The constant refrain was, "There is little you can do."

That was unacceptable. The tide turned the moment we decided to trust our own instincts and abilities. We chose to focus on the opportunity. We believed we could build something of significance if we could just sort through all the debris. Our first step was to commit to a path; the second, and most important, was to "see the end from the beginning," without limits. The stakes were high and there was no roadmap. The business had to be closed, inventory liquidated, and administrative issues resolved. Additionally, the historic commercial property was in desperate condition. Even more sobering was the loss of income, mounting healthcare costs, and nonexistent estate planning.

Despite overwhelming circumstances, we formulated a plan of action and made a leap into uncharted waters. We pledged to support each other regardless of the ups and downs, and we sought guidance in silencing our fears and doubts. We were familiar with normal business frustrations, but this was our mother and father. We could not let them down.

Through mutual encouragement, listening to inspirational speakers, upbeat music, exercise, and good nutrition, we prepared ourselves to succeed. By following proven techniques, we taught ourselves to think outside the box in order to recognize innovative solutions. Coincidentally, the mindset of "seeing the end from the beginning" is the same quality required in successful asset protection planning. This became a critical part of our strategy and brought everything into sharper focus. Suddenly, solutions appeared in the least likely places. We were amazed at how this apparent disaster could produce so many opportunities to change our lives, re-establish our roots, and connect with our future dreams. We were ultimately successful, but the experience led us in an unanticipated direction.

Repeatedly, we found our discussions recalling childhood stories revolving around a man revered by our grandfather. Papaw Chapman loved telling us stories of this man and always closed with "and I am a descendent of Johnny Appleseed." Then he'd point to the hand-carved statue of Johnny standing by the bay window watching over the farm and its many trees. These stories were unforgettable and they endured within us. It was no accident that we were recalling these stories, indeed it was our destiny. Johnny Appleseed Chapman was a part of us and we needed to know more.

Our research led us to Joe Besecker, director of The Johnny Appleseed Society at Urbana University. His enthusiasm and knowledge of all things "Johnny" is exceptional. His and others' efforts have resulted in the largest collection of historical documents, books, and memorabilia in the world on Johnny's life. Johnny is commonly believed to have been an eccentric wanderer with a penchant for planting apple trees. We found there was more to the man than the myth. His interests included religion, education, ecology, commerce, and wellness, coinciding with values we wished to uphold. As if by magic, we were finding ourselves attracting and being attracted to other people who shared our enthusiasm for Johnny's example. We met people like Jeff Meyer of American Forests, Ken Roberts of Johnny Appleseed LLC, and Robert Smith of the National Arbor Day Foundation, who are all ardent environmentalists and supporters of The Johnny Appleseed Society. We learned that a member of our Mastermind Group was an active supporter of healthy living and wellness education. He produces a TV program, magazine, and radio program to educate people on healthy lifestyle issues. He is also very interested in Johnny Appleseed.

Convinced that the possibilities were endless, we decided to make yet another leap. We embarked on the path to incorporate Johnny Appleseed into our business strategy and to form a nonprofit organization called Plant a Seed. We decided to undertake activities consistent with the philosophy and inspiration of Johnny. Johnny was a gatherer and planter of seeds, and we too will "plant a seed" in all that we do. One of our goals is to plant one million Johnny Appleseed trees. It is amazing what happens when you set big goals and think big thoughts. You can imagine our surprise upon meeting Mark Victor Hansen (coauthor of the *Chicken Soup for the Soul* book series) and finding we share similar goals. He too has a commitment to plant trees to reforest the planet.

We found the energy is in the path; we are on our way to achieving our goal to plant one million Johnny Appleseed trees.

We discovered a disaster, recognized an opportunity, and refused to acknowledge our doubts and fears. In return, we gained the opportunity to transform our imaginations into reality, celebrate our heritage, and exceed our wildest dreams.

"Everyone thinks that the principle thing to the tree is the fruit, but in point of fact, the principle thing to it is the seed."
—Friedrich Wilhelm Nietzsche

Denny Lane and Debra Lane Wright
Phone: (617) 487-9630
Email: The_Appleseed@fastmail.fm

⋈

Let's look at *your* current situation. Is there something that would improve your life or make you happier each day? What's preventing you from achieving this objective? What would it take for you to truly commit to achieving it?

Let us ask you this critical question: If you knew 100 percent that your efforts would result in the outcome you desire, would you invest your time and energy? Stated another way: would you do it if you knew you couldn't fail? Of course you would! Why then do the majority of people never achieve their desires? For starters, most never even take the time to set definitive clear objectives. But what about the ones who do? They lose faith along the way. Remember, faith is an essential prerequisite for success. With any goal or objective, you cannot allow daily obstacles or negative feedback by those around you to weaken your faith or focus.

How do you strengthen faith? By continuously feeding and strengthening your mind! Only you are in control of your future actions. Only you are responsible for a life of plenty or a life of mediocrity. It's your choice. It sounds simple but so many fail because they allow others to deter them and weaken their faith.

Dr. David Luquette's story is a well-written example of going forward in life asking: "What would I do if I could not fail?"

STEP BY STEP

Dr. David Luquette

If you had no time or money barriers what would you absolutely love to do?

My friend asked me this question. It changed my life. She then said, "See that wand sitting on the table? It's for you. Go ahead, pick it up." My stomach was in knots. What would I do if I had no barriers? The room was quiet and peaceful. Her voice was soothing and encouraging. The wand was twinkling at me as if to say, "I already know what you would do but I want you to say it yourself." I needed the courage to admit what I wanted and to expect I would be able to achieve it. Why was I hesitating? What would it really take to live the life I truly desired? How could I make it a reality? I continued looking at the wand, moving it up and down, watching the blue gel move through the clear cylinder carrying the twinkling stars. Finally, I blurted it out, "A chiropractor! I want to be a chiropractor!" At that moment I knew I would be a chiropractor. No more excuses. No more settling. No more confusion.

I knew I had to make it happen or I would live my life without ever being satisfied or fulfilled. Instantly the doubts set in. How could I tell my wife, my parents, and my friends that I would be quitting a good job and returning to school? I became absorbed with asking God powerful questions and looking for answers. As I imagined the responses to my news, I felt myself retreating to the safety of excuses as to why it was a bad idea to follow my dream.

Ring, ring. There it was. The telephone call that would change my life. "David, I think I had a wreck."

"What do you mean you 'think' you had a wreck?" I said.

It was my wife on the telephone. I quickly realized she was in shock and had just been in a car accident. I was out of town for my job and never felt so helpless. This event solidified the need for a dramatic change in my life.

I know the feeling all too well of being in a major car accident. I felt my wife's current confusion my first year of college when I had a car accident of my own. I sat in the hospital for hours before a stranger realized that I was in shock and that I had wandered in from the street. The hospital staff then treated me, stitched up my head, and sent me on my way. Two days later I was back and spent a week under constant supervision due to a concussion they had missed. They also told me I would require back surgery. This I declined, as I knew it would end my football career.

I suffered years of horrific pain in my legs, arm, and back. Finally a friend at work recommended a chiropractor. This recommendation altered the rest of my life. After treatment I was able to resume an active lifestyle I thought was gone forever.

I knew this past success in my personal life would assist my wife with her current accident. After rushing to be by her side, I learned of the multiple medications that were being recommended for her injuries. Without these "essential" medications, we were told, her life would be drastically compromised. My mission became more solidified than ever. Passion emerged from these accidents. We sought the quality natural healing care I knew would heal her and restore her ability to live pain-free.

The years of schooling were beyond challenging. Every fiber of my being wanted to quit and return to that safe, secure job I once knew. However my passion to learn the science of natural healing would not be denied. I am proud that I persevered and earned my Doctor of Chiropractic degree.

Starting my own private practice was a scary endeavor. However, my drive to share my knowledge with patients made every step exciting and rewarding. My desire to effectively communicate and treat people of all ages and conditions led to thousands of new patient referrals.

My mission statement is proudly displayed in every room of my clinic:

I am committed to communicating the art, science and philosophy of chiropractic both on an individual and global basis. I acknowledge the devastating effects of the lack of health on the human spirit and potential. I acknowledge God's presence in my life and in all my endeavors. I envision a world of optimum health and great human potential. My goal is to eliminate mediocrity and promote the reality of living a productive and inspired life. My perspective in life is not to let my good get in the way of my better.

I am celebrating ten years of successful practice. Eighty-five percent of my patients are referred by current patients. A patient can pay me no higher compliment than the honor of allowing me to treat a beloved family member or friend.

Thanks to God, my vision, family, patients, friends, a no-nonsense business manager, and staff, I enjoy a practice that is in the top 3 percent of the nation. Each and every day is more exciting and rewarding. When you unconditionally allow your life to accept the unlimited potential of the human spirit, the opportunities to help others, while achieving everything you personally desire, are limitless.

The West is going through an amazing shift in attitudes regarding healthcare. We are experiencing a wellness revolution. I am basking in its glory. My education in natural healing places me on the cutting edge of today's healthcare system, attracting patients who desire optimal health rather than the mere cover-up of symptoms. My colleagues and I now embark on revolutionary new stem cell research that utilizes the body's own tissue for natural healing.

We welcome you to learn more about our mission of "achieving and inspiring worldwide constant and never-ending achievement" online at: http://www.worldwidecani.com.

Each morning I awake and live the day knowing:

Before you can believe something you must think it is possible.

Once you think it is possible, you must believe you can accomplish it.
Once you know you can accomplish it, you must live it.
Once you live it, you know it.
Once you know it, you own it.
Once you own it—*you are unstoppable.*

Dr. David Luquette
Phone: (936) 371-0083
Email: davidluquette@cox.net

CR&CR

As you can see, individuals will take on massive undertakings if they have faith. We see this constantly in all types of business. We also see those who stand by in fear.

We deal heavily in professional forms of income diversification. In today's economy it is essential to have multiple streams of income. One of our endeavors involves a rock-solid business one can begin for less than two hundred dollars. This very business has already proven to generate millions of dollars in personal commissions for those who have actively participated. Some people however, many of whom are in dire need of additional income, will not invest two hundred dollars to begin this business. If we had a brand new car, completely paid for, and told these same people we would give it to them for two hundred dollars, they would find this money in a heartbeat. Why? Because they have zero doubt they could sell the car for more than two hundred dollars. On the other hand, they do not have the *faith* that they can turn their two-hundred-dollar business investment into hundreds of thousands, even millions of dollars. It's not the money—it's their faith!

How can an individual possibly achieve a higher standard of living if they don't have the faith in themselves that they can do so? The answer is they can't! The world is filled with good intentions. Good intentions get you nowhere. Again, you must first be willing. Then you must have the faith you can achieve your objective. Then you must have 100 percent focus. Never deviate from your objective. Then you must apply the necessary actions (practice) until your objective is achieved—allowing nothing to stand in your way.

Let's read this excellent story by our coauthor Dr. Tim Brady about how he achieved his dream by staying focused on the end result. Instead of starting a practice where it was sure to succeed and "someday" retiring to where he wanted to be, he simply went where he wanted to be and focused on making it work. Unconditional, leap of faith, total focus.

START OUT WHERE YOU WANT TO END UP

Dr. Tim Brady

1978: The blue spruce dominated my peripheral vision. The giant monoliths all pointed to the clean cerulean sky of the crystal clear Colorado morning. As I inhaled deeply I marveled at the rich scent of pine that filled my nostrils. The mountain stream sang its happy refrain as it danced past the tidy cabin that had sheltered me the last couple of nights as a guest of Buck Dean of the T Lazy 7 Ranch. The day would bring a trip on horseback to the base of the Maroon Bells, those lovely striated granite faces that watch over this verdant valley, as wise grandparents oversee their brood.

That night I had discovered Buck's album *Nashville Skyline*, by Bob Dylan and had revisited it several times. Buck had created a bathing spot in the cabin that was formed from a horse trough. The water entered it by cascading down a rock wall and filled the trough with the run-off. The propane lamps created a warm glow throughout the two rooms that warmed the heart as well. The wood burning stove kept the place toasty, taking the chill off the cool mountain nights. The cabin was a homebuilt work of art that formed its own home deep within my soul and produced fruit years later.

As "Girl from the North Country," a duet with Bob Dylan and Johnny Cash, resonated through my head, I gave thanks to God for the opportunity to stay in and experience a place that seemed so magical to me. Could it be possible that I could live here where I loved to vacation? Could I build a chiropractic practice in Colorado, where I could get sick people well and make a living surrounded by all this beauty?

I will be twenty-eight years old next month and graduate from Logan College of Chiropractic in January of 1978. Is it possible that I will be able to live in the playground where I love to climb, camp, ride horses, and ski? The smells alone beckon me and I feel closer to God here. I pray Lord that if this is where you want me to be, we make it happen together.

September 2004

The long view to the far blue horizon is spectacular. The brilliant gold, yellow, and orange aspen form an exquisite contrast with the large, deep green Douglas fir. One ridge overlaps another as you first are drawn in by the light blue sagebrush and olive green tufts of tall grass on the steep hillside that rapidly descends into the forest leading to the willow creek draw one thousand feet below and then gradually ascends up the far valley, pointing the way to the alpine plateau. No roads, rooftops, or wires are visible through the entire expanse of the vista.

The autumn colors take your breath away, both for their extreme beauty and what they signify as they indicate the winding down of another labor-of-love season constructing the B Lazy R. As I sit on the deck taking in the view, I find gratification in the work performed on the cabin this season and what has been accomplished over the last nine years. This has been a two-family project. Four adults and five children have been working to create a fabulous getaway on a secluded ridge at the end of a one and one-quarter-mile private road. The youngest of the children is now sixteen the oldest twenty-two.

The green metal roof protects a fifteen-hundred-square-foot, two-story log cabin made with trees spot cut from the surrounding hillsides, benches, and draws. Nestled on the high ridge, the cabin is built from Engelmann pine, Douglas fir, sub alpine, and aspen. The full round logs are hand-peeled, saddle-notched, and chinked inside and out.

Our two families have managed to work together two consecutive weeks and several long weekends each year over the last nine years to create the B Lazy R. The B is for Brady and the lazy R is for the Roberts, our next-door neighbors in Grand Junction, Colorado.

The cabin is functional and usable, but not yet finished. We probably have three to four more years until completion. It is not the final product but the process that has been of utmost importance to us as a family.

Principle: practice where you want to live.

I can count so many blessings in building my practice where I wanted to live. My heart is filled and nurtured by my surroundings.

By living and practicing where I wanted to be, I have been able to focus on shaping my practice to approach the fruition of my dreams. This focus and commitment has also provided me with an exceptional place to raise my children.

The path of chiropractic practice has a large heart to it. Helping people get well using techniques that involve no drugs or surgery is very rewarding and edifying. A profession where you touch people's lives and improve their wellbeing has truly enriched my life.

Following this path in Grand Junction, Colorado, has been the foundation of a long, solid career.

Dr. Tim Brady
Brady Chiropractic Group, PC
51428 1/4 Road
Grand Junction, CO 81501

CREESCR

Do you have the faith to start at the end point?

Do you have faith in your abilities? What could you accomplish in life if you applied willingness, faith, focus, and practice and combined them with the true secret to success?

What's the secret to success? Are you ready for life-changing information? Are you ready to apply a guaranteed success formula to all aspects of your life?

The four-part secret of success:
1. Do Something!
2. If it works—keep doing it
3. If it doesn't work—stop doing it!
4. Do something more!

Many state this is too simple to be accurate. We challenge you to prove us wrong. What do most people do? Basically nothing.

Those who do something often fall short of their objective, but repeat it because it is safer than doing something more that might achieve their original objective. They "settle" for what they got. This error leads to an endless routine of mediocrity and avoids step number four. In other words, they don't do anything new.

We can't make this any easier: If something is not leading you to successful achievement of a clearly defined objective—stop doing it! If it is working—keep doing it! But always remember—always continue your path to higher achievement by doing something new! Don't allow your life to fall into an endless routine of mediocrity!

Always remembering this simple four-step system and applying it to every area of your life will enhance your life beyond your wildest dreams.

Bring on metanoia factor #10!

METANOIA FACTOR 10

Beliefs result in tunnel vision

It's your personal decision whether this moves you closer to, or further away from, your desired life.

Your beliefs affect every aspect of your life. Let's take a simple example of a woman who has experienced less-than-desirable relationships with men.

Perhaps this woman was physically or verbally abused in numerous previous relationships. From these experiences she has created a belief system that "men are scumbags—they cannot be trusted."

This belief system, on the surface, may not appear to drastically affect her entire future, but let's further analyze the impact of this and other beliefs.

1. Beliefs cause us to see things in a very distinct manner.
2. Seeing things a distinct way causes us to *feel* a certain emotional response.
3. As discussed before, we *act* based on emotions, therefore, this causes us to act a specific way.
4. Because what we *get* is based on how we act. This belief ultimately is in total control of what we get in life.

See/Feel/Act/Get

Want to change what you get in life? Understanding your beliefs and changing them is key.

Let's look at the woman discussed above. Now, it is easy to understand why, when she sees a man approaching her in a shopping mall, she sees a scumbag. Her belief is that men are scumbags so there is no other way for her to see the man approaching. He may in fact be a very nice man. It is impossible for her to see any differently until she looks at and alters her belief system.

Next, let's look at how she feels. Perhaps threatened, angry, or repulsed?

How then might she act? Avoidance, anger, or confrontational?

What does she therefore get? Most certainly not a smile, a nice conversation, a rewarding relationship, nor even the love of her life!

Not only is she left with nothing, she probably believes the situation that just took place actually supports her belief system—"See, another one just like the rest!"

Let's say time passes and gradually her hurt begins to subside. She decides to reanalyze her belief that all men are scumbags. After some thought, she decides that just as there are good children and bad children, good doctors and bad doctors, good business people and bad business people, good women and bad women, this must also hold true for men. This results in a new belief system: there are good men and bad men.

Now that her belief system has changed, she sees things differently. Now when she sees a man she sees the possibility that he is a good man!

Now when a man approaches her in a mall she sees a prospect!

How does this make her feel? Not angry or repulsed. Instead she feels hopeful, curious, or even excited!

How does she therefore act? She doesn't want to avoid this man or be confrontational. She perhaps smiles, or initiates a conversation.

What does she get? A return smile, a rewarding conversation, a new friend, or the love of her life! The possibilities are endless!

Can you see how one belief system can affect so much?

Still not convinced that your beliefs rule your entire life?

You are walking down the street. As a man passes you, he slaps you across your head. Your belief is that people should never lay their hands on another person—especially unprovoked!

What do you see? A violent man.

What do you feel? Anger and the need for revenge.

How do you act? You prepare to fight!

What do you get? An angry rush of adrenaline and increased blood pressure.

As you turn to hit the man you realize he has fallen to the ground and is having an epileptic seizure.

Now what do you see? Someone in need!

Now how do you feel? Sympathetic.

Now how do you act? Call for help or assist with first aid.

Now what do you get? Hopefully the satisfaction of having saved someone's life!

There is no such thing as reality. Your reality is based on your belief system. If your belief is that this man hit you in a confrontational manner, the reality is you would retaliate by hitting him back in anger.

However, if your belief is that this man is in need of help, the reality is you would offer assistance.

Same circumstances—drastically different realities!

One of the fastest methods to change your life is to look at, analyze, and alter belief systems that are resulting in your current reality.

It is senseless to attempt changing your life without first changing your belief systems. Controlling your destiny starts with controlling your mind. What beliefs are holding you back? Time to take a serious look into your thought processes. The second you start analyzing your belief systems is the second your reality will change.

Our coauthor Dr. Greg Nelson, DC, CCSP, CSCS, understands the principle of *changing your mind first* to change your life.

THE BOUNCE-BACK-ABILITY FACTOR

Dr. Greg Nelson
DC, CCSP, CSCS

You know, it's funny—there isn't any noise to let you know you're there. You'd think there would be a crash, thud, maybe even a splat. But nothing really happens to let you know when you've officially hit bottom.

There was a day in my life, in the not too distant past, where all of the "victim" questions seemed to be on the tip of my tongue. Why me? What did I do to deserve this? I'm a nice guy. Why won't anyone help me? Why can't I ever seem to get my head above water? Survival has always been easy for me, why is success so difficult? The questions went on and on relentlessly in my mind.

We've all heard these questions and, in fact, we all know the answers, at least somewhere deep inside. The trick is admitting that we know the answers. Well, there is one more trick, infinitely more difficult, and that is doing something about those answers.

I had done a multitude of good things in my life—up until it happened. I had gone to school, studied hard, had my share of fun, and received a degree to play doctor for the rest of my life. I didn't need the doctor title or prestige, I just wanted to finally achieve the level of success we all deep down feel we deserve.

After graduation, I worked with a doctor in Illinois. I had worked for him through the majority of my schooling and it seemed only natural to work with him as an associate after I received my degree. That's exactly what I did, at least in title. I had no direction and no patients of my own. After seven months, I realized it was time to go. This just wasn't my "plan." At that time what I failed to realize was that I had no plan. I just knew my current situation wasn't working.

For no apparent reason, San Antonio, Texas beckoned. When I decided it was time to go, I didn't have a job to go to or a place to live. I had no family in town. I didn't know *anybody* there. I couldn't even find the Alamo. It was perfect! I have always been impulsive but to just "up and go" was even out of character for me. I'm outgoing, but reserved. Impulsive, but rational. Simply put, I can easily jump into something as long as I know I have the upper hand. At that point, San Antonio had the upper hand. It's where I felt I *had* to be.

My shadow first graced my new home on December 28. By June 1, I met the woman who would be my wife. By November 22, I purchased my first practice. By December 6, I was engaged to be married. That was a whirlwind of a year!

Whew! Within twelve months I had turned my world completely upside-down and established some pretty serious roots.

My universe was literally perfect, on the outside, but I couldn't shake the questions still stirring in my mind.

Is this right? Did I make the right decision? Should I have put more thought into moving to San Antonio? Is owning a practice right for me?

I didn't know if I had done the right things for the right reasons. I certainly didn't want to bring a new wife down with me if I hadn't. The pressure was building to a critical level.

Since high school, my pressure release valve has been golf. I love being outdoors with nothing more than the next shot to challenge me. It is a wonderful way to forget the troubles of the world for a few hours.

One day, all of a sudden, even golf couldn't stop the feeling of impending doom. I couldn't silence the voice asking the questions. I wasn't having fun. I couldn't relax. I walked off the course.

About the time my trunk slammed shut I reached bottom. A total failure. I was ready to give it all up. I didn't even know what that meant, but I was afraid I was going to find out. Maybe afraid is not the word—I was so depressed I couldn't truly be afraid.

We have all heard the saying that it is darkest just before the dawn. I learned that lesson that day. It was at the same moment that I hit the lowest point that my survival mechanism kicked in, and I knew my life would have to be different. There was no alternative.

The simplicity and beauty of this life is that if you expect something to be different, and control your focus, you can create the outcome you want.

First came acceptance. I had to accept that it was time to do something new. I could not simply repeat my actions and expect a different result in my life. After all, those actions got me to exactly where I was. So, I started doing things that would change my world.

For simplicity sake, I decided to change everything without *physically* changing anything. Instead I changed my perspective and focused my intent to ensure I was on purpose with each action I took. I decided to live in the "now" moment rather than the scary "what if" of the future. I found that living "now" and not fearing "later" was far easier than how I had lived my life to date.

When my practice rapidly doubled I knew I was on track. My focus was strong. I didn't use gimmicks or advertising. I didn't "do" anything differently. I just became different. I felt different and acted different. This attitude quickly became contagious. It drew people to me, professionally and personally. What I had created, without realizing it, was a magnet for all things good.

Today good things seem to roll in effortlessly. I am so far from the bottom that I couldn't possibly find my way back. How can you go where your mind cannot conceive?

The questions have stopped echoing in my head. I am on track. Everyday begins a new chapter better than the last.

So this story ends with "Once upon a time."

Once upon a time, my universe wasn't all that I thought it was supposed to be. The little voice said all I had to do was open my heart and mind and *do something* about it.

Live in the moment to control your future destiny. What is your little voice telling you to do?

Dr. Greg Nelson, DC, CCSP, CSCS
San Antonio, TX
Email: dsportsdc@sbcglobal.net

ॐ☯ॐ

Bring on metanoia factor #11

Creating the proper subconscious pictures is the easy way to have what you want in life

How many times do you have situations arise when you state to yourself, "I don't know what to do"?

Would you like to know how to solve any situation? In order to do so you must become fully in tune with the situation in order for your mind to effectively evaluate your options. You must open your mind to the many possibilities available to you; this creates awareness. You are then aware of the situation and your options. Now simply focus on the ones that are most viable.

By opening your mind you become intuitive to your surroundings. Information that would typically go unnoticed is now captured and utilized.

Example: Let's say you are a dentist flipping through a newspaper. You are quickly scanning the pages and the word *dentist* jumps off the page at you. Have you ever had this experience when a topic is on your mind? There are thousands of words on each newspaper page—how does one word jump out at you? This is your "magic genie" working for you—your subconscious mind. This is a powerful sector of your brain that sees all and hears all. Your conscious mind intellectualizes what is important and what is not. Subjects of great interest or concern are stored in your subconscious mind along with emotion. This emotional component causes your subconscious mind to constantly scan all sensory input for additional information on this subject. Hence the word *dentist* jumps into your conscious mind and you become aware of its presence.

Taking the time to clearly understand what is most important to you, and why, will provide the emotion to properly store it in your subconscious. This awareness of how important the subject is to you causes your subconscious mind to constantly scan all information in your surroundings for the people, resources, and information needed to bring your desires to fruition. In short, you receive answers to achieving your objectives.

Scheduling the first corporate client for our company Power Strategies, http://www.appliedmotivation.net is the perfect example—Dr. Talcott tells the story:

In 1984, my first book, *Balance—Your Key to Happy, Healthy, Productive Living*, was published.

In this book I covered in detail how your mind finds solutions once you are open to receiving them. Over the years there have been countless occasions where I have heard individuals say a certain word and my subconscious mind has instantly brought it to my attention. You see, if I wasn't open to receiving information on these important topics, these opportunities to gain new information, resources, or personal relationships would simply pass me by. To illustrate, I have heard people talking in restaurants dozens of times about something that was of interest to me. I was made aware of my interest in these conversations by hearing distinct individual words throughout their discussion. This is how I booked our first corporate client. I was sitting in a restaurant and overhead a woman talking about a multidisciplinary healthcare clinic. My subconscious mind picked up the word "chiropractic." There was no way I could hear the entire conversation, but the key words were very clear to me. My subconscious mind was hearing all and seeing all.

Your conscious mind blocks the majority of sensory input. These key words were picked up by my subconscious mind, and since I was open to accepting this information, they were brought to the attention of my conscious thought processes.

I then heard the word "osteopath," then the word "medical." My genie (subconscious mind) is always zeroed in on words that are important to me and my life plan.

When I finished my meal I stood up and said to the women, "You must be in the healthcare field." This led to a pleasant conversation. I learned she was the wife and office manager of an osteopath who had a large expanding practice. Their staff/employee group was in desperate need of our services.

We exchanged information and they became a client the following week. This all came from the genie being aware and constantly scanning my surroundings for information, resources, and people that can bring me closer to my personal goals and ambitions. How incredibly powerful and exciting!

C3☙)C3

Situations like this are around us each and every day.

Do you clearly and concisely understand what is most important to you and why?

Is your mind open and aware, ready to receive pertinent information, resources, and personal relationships from your everyday surroundings? Once information or opportunities are presented to you, are you ready to capitalize on them?

Was I ready to act? Yes. I simply initiated a polite conversation with a woman who I knew had common interests! It's really that simple! What would most people have done? Walked away and gained absolutely nothing.

The next question to ask yourself to assist in gaining awareness is, "Am I focusing on the past or future?" Most spend their lives focused on past events. This is like replaying a DVD and hoping for a different ending. Are past issues or experiences holding you back? If so, we have exciting news for you! Remember we stated that there is no such thing as reality. Reality is solely your perception of certain events. This creates a picture in your mind and ultimately dictates how you feel about an occurrence. The exciting fact is you can change these pictures of past reality in order to break through mental obstacles preventing you from achieving future goals and ambitions!

Accomplishing this is as simple as "repainting" new pictures for your mind to hold to replace the current pictures holding you back. Remember, even your current pictures are not reality. Therefore, after successfully mastering this technique, you can paint whatever reality is required to progress forward to an exciting new and prosperous life!

You must understand that your subconscious mind does not judge things as being good, bad, real, imagined—in your subconscious mind things just are. Your conscious mind makes judgments and attaches emotions. It then stores them in the subconscious. Like a computer—garbage in, garbage out.

The pictures that are stored in your subconscious mind are individually tied to a specific emotion. This greatly affects the way you react to situations, and the way you act determines what you get in life.

Therefore, do you want to change what you get? You must then change the pictures in your subconscious mind to the type that will allow you to progress and act in a proactive manner. They should always move you toward your clearly defined objectives.

This essential process allows you to break free from repetitive actions and routines that ultimately result in mediocrity or failure.

Would you like new people in your life to assist you in accomplishing higher objectives? Then paint a new picture in your mind of the type of people you wish to meet, including the characteristics you desire.

Here's another example. If you really want to be a better golfer you will paint a picture of an individual who is exceptional at golf. Your new picture will allow your subconscious mind to constantly be scanning your surroundings for individuals who fit this picture. Once your subconscious mind identifies an individual who fits this picture, it will bring this to the attention of your conscious mind. The next step? You must be willing and ready to take action and initiate a conversation, etc. You must be ready to act when new information, resources, and people are presented to you!

Our coauthor Dr. Eddie Rettstatt knows how to reprogram.

FORGIVING IS FOR GIVING YOU
BETTER HEALTH

Dr. Eddie Rettstatt

Each day we either increase the state of our health or allow ourselves to produce disease.

We are born with our own individual energy field. It is complete in our first cell and replicates with each cell thereafter. It is "God" presence. My core belief in this supreme omnipotent energy source is born out in responses I see in patients during their care.

This energy causes the body to function as a perfect unit, but that function is directly affected by the elements of lifestyle we choose—including our thought "habit patterns."

For the body to respond optimally in health and wellness, it must be in an alkaline state. As it becomes more acid, it is negatively affected. In this acidic environment, protection for our survival is top priority and energy for healing is not available. The main creators of an unhealthy acidic state are: improper diet, lack of proper hydration, lack of exercise, lack of rest, lack of clean air, and most importantly lack of "thought control." Thoughts have the greatest impact on acidity.

Years of clinical practice have proven this to me and my patients.

The beginning of all disease is mental, emotional, and spiritual stress. They are always present before disease starts.

Harboring blame and holding onto old hurts is especially destructive; hence forgiveness gives forth healing.

We live in a society that constantly bombards us with negative energy. Negative mental images actually increase your body's acidity.

An acid body functions in a protection/survival mode. When alkaline, it is in a healing/thriving mode, but it can only function in one mode at a time. The objective is to move out of protection/survival and into healing/thriving.

Your thoughts are the strongest determinant of your acid/alkaline balance. Negative thoughts, such as fear, anger, worry, and distress, create a need for protection, while positive thoughts, such as love, joy, abundance, and forgiveness, result in health and growth.

The great news: you can change your thoughts. We all know you reap what you sow. What you put in your subconscious (sow in the soil) you shall see reflected in your life and health (reap the fruit). Therefore, the key is to control what you "plant" in your subconscious.

I learned firsthand how negative thoughts interfered with communication between my brain and tissue cells, keeping my body from being in touch with the intelligence that created it.

But how could I choose what to think?

I found I could replace the thoughts that reflect circumstances I *don't* want in my life with thoughts that reflect what I do want!

Anytime I am aware of a negative thought, I simply think or say: 1) "I cancel the thought I just had"; 2) "I forgive myself for allowing that thought"; and 3) "I am so thankful for [name something good]." The three optimum affirmations that I have found to use for number three are: "I am so thankful for perfect health, total happiness, and absolute success."

At that point my body turns toward an alkaline state.

I then found the most powerful way to return to a true state of health and happiness.

The power of forgiveness. The process of forgiveness removes the interference of healthy energy flow. The power of forgiveness is about replacing past negative thoughts with present-time thoughts of unconditional love. It cleanses subconscious memories while bringing body responses into real time versus reacting to past memories.

To use an example: I'm driving down the street. I am upset about an incident at the office. I get broadsided. My body tenses and goes into spasm—especially my neck. This is a protective response and was needed at the time. After the trauma is healed, this protective response is no longer needed. However, in my subconscious mind, the muscle spasms are tied to the memory of being upset. Now every time I am upset, my neck muscles go into spasm.

After understanding this, I wanted to "update that memory" so it no longer had control over my body. I found the best way was by expressing forgiveness. Forgiveness readily alkalizes the body and reverses the acidity caused by negative feelings.

Holding on and resisting instead of letting go throws the body into a nonhealing, chronic protective mode.

Holding on was affecting no one but me! The more I proclaimed it unfair, the more acidic I became. Giving up the desire to get even was the answer.

Dr. M.T. Morter Jr., my mentor, taught me the four steps of forgiveness. Anytime a conscious negative thought is related to another person, either think silently or speak the following four affirmations.

1. Forgive the other person. "I forgive [name the other person] and/or all others for anything, real or imagined, that they have done to me in any time, space, place, or dimension, that would cause a negative feeling that would be detrimental to my health." This is done totally nonjudgmentally. Whether the other person was right, wrong, good, or bad is irrelevant.

2. Give the other person permission to forgive me. "I give [name the other person] and/or all others permission to forgive me for anything, real or imagined, that I may have done to them in any time, space, place, or dimension, that would cause a negative feeling that would be detrimental to my health." This step is necessary to open the original energy path.

3. Forgive yourself. "I forgive myself for anything I need to be forgiven for, real or imagined, in any time, space, place, or dimension, that would cause a negative feeling that would be detrimental to my health." This is done so you don't replace the original negative memory with guilt.

4. Learn a lesson from the experience. "I must focus on the good, however small it may be. I want to learn something from everyone."

Use these four steps every time a negative thought related to another human being comes into your mind.

I challenge and encourage you to say these affirmations and practice forgiveness each night as you go to sleep. Let them be your last conscious thought.

Do this for thirty days and e-mail me your results.

You will be enjoying better health, more wealth, and increased happiness just like me.

Remember, forgiving is for giving you better health.

Dr. Eddie Rettstatt
Phone: (817) 228-4151
Email: erettstatt@aol.com

C3 ED CB

Reprogramming your subconscious mind is not a form of denial. It's a method to create a stronger, more efficient, and productive mind that is capable of attracting everything you require to truly thrive in life. Think of how powerful it would be to reprogram all past pictures of failure into new pictures of productive winning! Think of the new confidence this would create and the accelerated ability to attract the needed information, resources, and people into your life.

It is unclear to us why so many feel this is difficult or even impossible.

Some individuals overanalyze this process and state: "What about the real pictures I have in my mind—like what my old house used to look like?"

Have you ever returned to your childhood home? Most are amazed at how much smaller it appears. This is because your stored pictures are from the perspective of a child who was three (or more) feet shorter than you are today! It is not a current reality. It is your perspective of the way things were—*at the time.*

Can you start to see how nothing is truly real and that reality is nothing more than the pictures you choose to store in your mind taken from the perspective and emotional state you were in at the time?

You, and you alone, are the individual in control of these pictures. You can make these pictures work for you or against you. It's your choice!

Start making your mind work for you by changing your subconscious pictures to those that are advantageous to your future. The world can instantly become a much more rewarding, exciting, and prosperous place.

Bring on metanoia factor #12!

Metanoia Factor 12

Living your own life begins with releasing other people's 'shoulds'

As we proceed throughout the years of our lives, we build a vast storehouse of false beliefs. Beliefs that are not our own, but rather, belong to others. It is essential you take time to evaluate the many "shoulds" in your life and ensure they are actually your own.

Example:

"You should go to church on Sunday morning because Saturday night doesn't count."

"You should beat your kids or they will be spoiled."

"You should not beat your kids or you will screw them up for life."

Or most commonly:

"You should take your kids to Wal-Mart and beat them so we can all watch!"

You can start by examining six things you did yesterday, actions you took, people with whom you communicated, functions you performed, and ask: "Why did I do that?"

We are willing to wager that over half the time your reply is:

"I did it because I was supposed to," "I did it because it was the right thing to do," or some other form of "I should...."

Shoulds make us perform in specific ways. Shoulds rule our actions. Therefore, to live the life you want you must ask yourself:

"Is that *my* should?"
"Where did that should come from and why do I believe it?"

Our coauthor Teresa Luquette is an expert at helping others stop "shoulding" all over themselves.

SHOULD SHOULDN'T BE

Teresa Luquette

"I'm so sorry. That's so sad. I can't imagine not having a mother." That's the usual response I get when people learn that my mother died the day I was born. I nonchalantly reply, "I never really knew her so I don't feel bad about losing her."

One day my oldest sister heard me say, "I've never lost anyone." She responded, "Yes, you have, and one day you will mourn the loss of our mother."

The day my daughter Sarah was born everything changed. Holding my baby in my arms and experiencing an overwhelming unconditional mother's love took my breath away. The simultaneous joy of my newborn combined with emotions over the loss of my mother was powerful beyond words.

That's when the shoulds took up residency. I felt insecure and lonely. I truly felt I should have a mother. I needed a mother. Why was I deprived of a mother's love? How could a loving God take a child's mother?

I lay there sobbing. How ridiculous. I am an independent strong career woman. What was happening to me? I *should* have been happy and glowing.

I tried to work myself out of those feelings. All the things I told myself growing up weren't working. Where was my strength? My independence? Get it together girl! Suck it up! You *should* be strong. *Should* someone be telling me what I tell everyone else? "You're not a victim."

This journey began when I was blessed with the news I was expecting a baby. Wow! I couldn't believe it and neither could anyone else. I had been totally focused on myself, my career, and supporting my husband through medical school. Everyone, except God, knew a child was in the five-year plan, not the one-year plan. I'll never forget my sister's screech of excitement followed by, "Oh! Wow! This is not in your plan. I thought a baby was in the five-year plan."

At that time I was almost thirty and still not planning for a baby. Looking back, this was the true beginning of the shoulds. Everyone knew I *should* have a baby by now. We had been married ten years. Was something wrong? Could we have children? Why hadn't we?

The should journey from independent business women, to mother, to mompreneur has been nothing short of a Power Rangers morphing. I'm convinced the next generation of Power Rangers should be women morphing through the various stages of their lives.

I have been on the mompreneur track for eleven years. My oldest daughter will be twelve in May.

My second major morphing occurred after the birth of my second daughter, Anne.

From career woman, to traveling career woman with child, stay-at-home working mom, home school mom, and currently "mompreneur"—I have come to the realization that we are all right (alright). Women, that is, of course! Whether you are a mother, mompreneur, CEO, with or without children, a few children, lots of children, or home school mom, … you're okay! When I stopped shoulding myself, I was able to stop shoulding other women. I have learned to respect women with differences.

I no longer believe God *should* have given me a mother. I am grateful for *all* my mothers. So many women have mothered me. My sisters mothered me and still do. Even when I was mothering them, they were mothering me. I asked one of my sisters why she didn't slap me silly for all the unsolicited mothering advice I gave her before I had children. She said, "I knew you would figure it out for yourself someday." What a mom.

My "other" mothers, like my grandmothers, who gave unselfishly of themselves; my mother-in-law who has taught me unconditional love; my good friend Debbie who taught me girl stuff, like how to buy way too many shoes and too much make-up, what two-hundred-plus thread count is and how to buy the good stuff; another friend Debbie who taught me loyalty by example; and numerous teachers and mentors, including Oprah and *The Brady Bunch* mom.

I have been married for twenty years to my best friend, mentor, and life partner. We have two genius and incredible daughters, a dog, and a cat. Professionally, I specialize in development, management, and sales of companies, assets, and products. I am also involved in many philanthropic ventures, including supplying women business owners and prospective owners with training and resources. I serve on my daughters' school board and enjoy supporting education by helping schools meet their business and financial objectives so they can focus on education.

A friend and mentor of mine, Dr. Ty Talcott, posed this fill-in-the-blank question.

"If I died tomorrow it would all be a waste because I never got to _____."

If something jumps in the blank it is likely a true passion and probably your magnificent obsession. I call it the "should buster." Ty says, "If you're not doing something related to whatever jumps in the blank, then you're likely doing what you or others think you should be doing versus living your own life."

My blank was filled with "help others achieve their potential by sharing the principles and techniques that have made my life more enjoyable and successful." My passion is providing women with all the resources they need to be successful entrepreneurs or mompreneurs. You can visit my Web site at http://enlightenedgroup.com or e-mail me at teresa@enlightenedgroup.com. You'll find things like secrets to having it all and quick surveys to test your shoulds.

I've learned that it's a waste of time and talent to let shoulds get in my way. I am experiencing the joy and freedom in my life that only comes from fulfilling my destiny and doing what I was intended to do.

My hope is that all women will enjoy freedom from shoulding all over themselves while fulfilling their own unique noble purposes.

Teresa Luquette
Phone: (936)559-0500
Email: Teresa@enlightenedgroup.com

CRSOCR

As stated earlier, our beliefs, including shoulds, make us blind to anything contrary to them. If your core belief is that you are successful, you cannot see yourself in any other way. You become blind to, avoid, repulsed by, and even insulted by anyone who states or acts in a way that implies you are not successful.

The same is true if you feel you are a failure. If you truly believe you are a failure you will not accept, or act, on the many opportunities that could lead you to a very successful life. People will do almost anything to be right. If they feel they are a failure and actually acted on opportunities that could make them rich, they might actually become successful. If that happened, their beliefs that they are failures would be incorrect, and people would rather be right than rich! Therefore, if people think they are failures, their actions reflect this belief and they experience the outcome of these actions—failure.

Can you see how analyzing your belief systems and shoulds is essential to accomplishing your ultimate objectives in life?

Many of your personal objectives are in fact based on other people's shoulds. As an example, your parents may have told you: "You should graduate from high school, go to college, get a degree, then get a secure job." Is this really *your* objective? There is nothing wrong with this if it actually is *your* objective. The key is ensuring that you are living *your* life—not the life of someone else!

If you do not take the time to analyze the shoulds in your life, the result is leading a life of buried bitterness, resentment, and unhappiness. Take time to reflect on the shoulds in your life. Once you do this, you will quickly realize how your life is being lived according to other people's belief systems. This is *your* life. The only way to be happy is to live it on your terms. Follow your own shoulds and eliminate those that don't work by applying the secret to success:

1) Do something (based on the should).
2) If it's working, keep doing it.
3) If it's not working—stop.
4) Do something new.

As long as you are applying this simple, powerful formula to your own shoulds, you will always be on the path to a happy, fulfilled life!

This metanoia factor will give you plenty to think about. Take the necessary time and identify your shoulds. How you live the rest of your life depends on it! Be sure you are living *your* life—it is the only one you have!

Bring on metanoia factor #13.

METANOIA FACTOR 13

Your daydreams lead to a new reality

Have you ever caught yourself daydreaming? What do these thoughts that race through your mind really mean? Daydreams are often thoughts of the way we wish things to be. Taking these random thoughts and enhancing them by forming a clear, concise picture can lead to dramatic changes in your reality through the formalized process of visualization.

The difference between random daydreams and visualization is twofold:

1) Clarity
2) Action

Enhancing your daydream by creating a highly definitive picture will allow your mind to initiate forces that attract the necessary resources to make your picture a reality. The only remaining factor is: will you take action? Is your picture simply a wish or is it something you really desire to bring into reality? The choice is yours. If you elect to act upon the resources your mind attracts to you, the universe will continue to mobilize unseen forces to assist you in accomplishing your desired objective. For these forces to be sustained you must hold your picture in high clarity and consistency.

This will change your random daydream into a powerful visualization process.

While holding the highly clarified picture in your mind, you must also block negative thought processes, such as doubt, that stop positive advancement toward your objectives.

You must also distance yourself from negative self images and shut down negative self-talk such as:

"I don't deserve it."
"I'm not smart enough."
"I'm not strong enough."
"I'm too old."
"I'm too young."

Are you starting to see how your mind can sabotage your life? These negative thoughts and images drastically hinder the power of the visualization process to achieve your desired outcome.

Negative thoughts or images held long enough create entire belief systems. As already covered, belief systems dramatically alter our actions. Our actions dramatically affect our outcome. Keeping your mind focused on positive, desired, highly clarified visualizations is essential to experiencing higher accomplishments.

Positive visualizations also create belief systems; however, these greatly enhance your life.

What daydreams do you have? Have you ever taken the time to analyze what is really important to you about these particular daydreams? By identifying the most desirable factors you can turn your daydreams into powerful high clarity visualizations that vastly enhance your life. Planned or scripted visualizations are the most powerful.

Follow this simple procedure to fully benefit from the power of visualizations.

1) Daydream about something for which you have a burning desire. This in no way needs to be a material object. It could be more free time or fun in your life.
2) Write down a description of this daydream.

3) Identify the most important parts of your description.

4) Turn these important parts into a few highly descriptive sentences of what you really want and how it would make you feel if you accomplished it. How will you feel? What will your friends say? Describe what you will look like. Are you laughing? Are you at peace and relaxed? Do you feel proud? Be very descriptive in every detail.

5) Now hold this clear picture and these feelings clearly in your mind. Repeat this descriptive process over and over again.

6) Tape-record yourself describing this new picture and your feelings in vivid detail. Play this recording over and over throughout your day.

7) Tape written reminders to "see" your visualization on your bathroom mirror, in your bedroom, on your refrigerator, etc.

This process will help ingrain your positive visualization clearly in your mind to initiate powerful forces for its achievement. As resources and opportunities are presented to you, ensure you immediately act upon them. Do not allow negative images and indecision to hold you back. All reality first begins with a simple thought or daydream. Before you go to the dry cleaner you first see yourself driving, picking up the clothes, and finally going home. Within minutes this thought or daydream becomes a reality. The dry-cleaned clothes are magically hanging in your closet. All this from a simple thought!

Start turning fantasy into reality each and every day. Use your mind to enhance your daydreams into powerful visualizations in order to create your ultimate life filled with happiness and prosperity.

Bring on metanoia Factor #14!

Your ability to obtain everything you want from life is directly proportional to the benefits your achievements create for others

In the introduction we talked about creating a team. With our Inner Circle we talk about "the team," and once again we will talk about the team—it is that important. In fact, life is simple: surround yourself with the right team and victory is yours!

It makes sense to surround yourself with the right people who possess the required knowledge, capital, contacts, resources, etc., needed to accomplish your objective—if you want victory!

Alone we have limited capabilities. A team however possesses exponential capabilities. What do you want to accomplish in life? Accomplishing it will depend on your ability to attract the appropriate people to assist you in the process.

Think about any great accomplishment you have made in your life. Now think about how many individuals assisted in the process. This could range from a salesperson who provided you the knowledge to purchase the needed office equipment, to a business partner who provided required insight or required knowledge, to a spouse or friend who assisted in the completion of other required tasks allowing you to focus your time and energies on the job at hand. Some of these individuals may not appear to be part of the core team that ultimately accomplished the objective, but they most certainly assisted with steps along the way.

Now envision developing the ability to fully communicate with those around you in order to formalize an efficient team, where each person knows their responsibilities, as well as their personal benefits when the objective is accomplished. These are key factors when developing a team:

Clear communication and an understanding of personal responsibilities.

Personal reward or benefit when the objective is accomplished.

The infrastructure to having everything you want in life, both personally and professionally, is the development of your "personal power team."

We are surrounded by many individuals in our lives—our family, friends, coworkers, etc. Realistically we cannot simply replace all of these individuals with new people who we feel are more beneficial to our objectives. The key is up-leveling those who are part of your current team while adding new members along the way!

But how do you start the process? How do you get other people to assist you in accomplishing your goals and objectives? How do you get others to play on your team?

The process begins by assisting each person currently part of your team in raising their knowledge and understanding of success principles. After all, how can you travel the road to greatness when surrounded by those who have no dream or aspiration of higher accomplishment? You can start this process by ensuring that each person on your team reads this book. Then, continue feeding your mind through educational/motivational books, CDs, seminars, and even social settings with other like-minded individuals. A powerful option available to you and your team members is our Inner Circle, a diversified group of individuals dedicated to personal development, wealth accumulation, and asset protection. Visit us online: http://www.themetanoiafactor.com.

As stated earlier, recruiting new people to your power team involves always being aware of the two-sided sign everyone wears on their forehead. This sign is constantly rotating with one side stating: "I'm important!" While the other side reads: "What's in it for me?"

It is essential to communicate to your team members, and potential team members, how important they are to the process and what their personal benefits will be when the objective is accomplished. Personal recognition and respect is critical in keeping your team constantly moving forward. Realizing and acting on this will put you ahead of most businesses, and individuals—people will flock to your team.

Why do some individuals stop responding to particular bonuses, rewards, or recognition over time? Their needs change! For this reason it is essential to understand that all people are motivated by four basic needs. Understanding where a particular person is on this scale at any given time will determine your ability to effectively lead your team to victory.

Level 1: Survival. If you are in a situation where you are afraid you will lose your house, not have enough food to feed your family, or even go bankrupt, your core focus is surviving. Whatever it takes to survive becomes an extreme motivator. If you are a dying man in the desert, you will do nearly anything for a glass of water.

Level 2: Belonging. Once your survival needs are met they are no longer your core motivator. That same man, once he has reached the oasis and has all the water he needs, will do little or nothing for a glass of water. It is no longer a motivator. When a person can turn their attention away from survival, they are now first motivated by love and belonging. They seek a mate or a group that provides them a feeling of belonging—a group that appreciates them and shares similar interests, goals, and desires.

Level 3: Recognition. Once an individual has both Level 1 and Level 2 needs met, their main motivation factor is to be recognized both within, and outside, the group.

Level 4: Self Actualization. As individuals progress up the hierarchy of human motivators, they reach a level where survival is no longer an issue. They are no longer driven by belonging or recognition, as these needs have also been fulfilled. Their main motivating factor is to become "all they can be." This often includes a new spiritual awareness or understanding.

The key in maximizing your team is understanding at which motivational level they reside and fulfilling that need for them. Remember, individuals will shift from one level to the next, both up and down. As an example, they may go through a divorce and instantly require an increased level of love and belonging, or they may have a financial setback and fall right back to Level 1. Be aware of those changes and assist them. You will generate undying loyalty.

As Dick Vermeil, general manager and football coach of the Super Bowl St. Louis Rams, said:

"Winning is not complicated. People complicate it. If you surround yourself with the right people, *you win*."

We surround ourselves with the right people and want to thank you for your time and thank our coauthors for their contributions to this book. We look forward to seeing you in the Inner Circle or at a seminar in the near future.

Appendix A

A metanoia for employers: someone knows what would increase your sales and create a more efficient and happy team

What would it mean to you and your business if someone knew and shared with you the specific top ten things you could do to increase sales to your customers, clients, or patients? And further...knew the top ten things that could increase employee retention, improve morale, and increase production?

Someone does! It should be no surprise that it is your employees.

The challenge is that they will not tell you.

We have proven techniques that get them to tell us!

At Power Strategies Inc. we unleash human potential in individuals and turn ordinary employee groups into power teams to accomplish your business goals and objectives.

Our customized seminars bring out the best in your employees and ultimately in your business.

Our unique methods are designed to optimize employee productivity, efficiency, and cooperation.

After all, your business is your employees. We use a unique seminar and teaching system that is aimed at assisting your employees to realize what they want from life and how to go about getting it. During our seminar your employees realize the seminar is truly about them.

Your employees appreciate the fact that you as the employer took the initiative to provide them the ability to accomplish more in their personal and professional lives. We teach them that the way for the team to stay together is for the business to prosper. For these two reasons, they are much more willing to assist you in achieving your business goals and objectives.

During the seminar we:
1. Raise employee self-esteem.
2. Assist employees in understanding how to acquire their personal goals and desires.
3. Produce a safe, interactive environment that gains employee trust. (This in turn allows Power Strategies to clarify how accomplishing their personal goals and desires is dependant on a secure income stream and stable work environment.)
4. Obtain invaluable employee feedback through an anonymous system, allowing us to gather information that would never be revealed to management due to fear of embarrassment, inadequacy, or retribution.

The vast majority of employees, regardless of the particular business they work for, feel greatly underappreciated. They feel like they have no significant impact on their daily work environment and that management just doesn't care.

Our seminar puts your employees on your side and gets them excited about being part of a growing, secure company that cares about their personal goals, ambitions, and daily work environment.

The result of each employee's mental transition is a significant step toward taking your company to the next level of efficiency and profitability.

What this means is that with the assistance of Power Strategies Inc., your business can have "It."

What Is "It"?

"It" is providing your staff/employee team with the proper mental foundation, combined with an understanding of the **science of applied motivation**, that will perpetuate your business far beyond the competition.

Without "It"—you cannot succeed.
With "It"—you cannot fail.

Our magnificent obsession is to teach others the proven principles we have utilized to produce the highest levels of personal and business success.

If you are serious about reaching higher business success and profitability, Power Strategies makes the process simple and stress-free.

Step #1: Schedule a private seminar event for you and your staff by calling 469-355-6036.

Step #2: Complete step-by-step pre-seminar forms.

Step #3: Enjoy a relaxing, informative, life-changing seminar with Power Strategies.

Step #4: Receive invaluable staff feedback reports from Power Strategies.

Step #5: Benefit from efficient, effective follow-up reports and updates prepared for you and your staff.

Step #6: Implement suggestions from reports and updates.

Step #7: Witness dramatic staff member and work environment enhancements.

Step #8: Watch your business prosper!

Following these proven steps will allow you to achieve the highest levels of business success. Your staff members will be happier, more productive, and efficient. The result is a work environment consisting of problem-solvers instead of problem-causers.

Life Is Short—Prosper

Appendix B

What is your personal story of victory?

If you have a story of victory or triumph or have achieved success from the implementation of a specific success "rule," you may be interested in participating in our next book.

Or better yet ...

Do you have a special story? Would you like to have your story included in the book and have your picture on the back cover?

Would that be of benefit to your credibility with existing or prospective patients, customers, or clients?

Would that help differentiate you from the pack?

Or just be fun for family and friends?

It can be a reality!

For more information e-mail
talcott@buildingincome.com
or call Power Strategies Inc. at
(469) 762-8026
Visit our Web site:
http://www.appliedmotivation.net

For more information on Power Strategies Inc. products, customized seminars, or the Inner Circle, call 469-762-8026 or visit them online at http://www.appliedmotivation.net.

For consumer copies of this book visit http://www.barnesandnoble.com Or http://www.amazon.com Or http://www.wheatmark.com. Quantity orders or special edition orders can be purchased by calling (469) 762-8026 or emailing talcott@buildingincome.com.

You may also fax this page with credit card information to (720) 559-8001.

Order form for consumers only, one to five books.

Payable in U.S. funds only. Book price = $19.95 U.S. and $24.95 Canada per book plus $3.00 per copy postage and handling (to a maximum of $9.00 postage and handling).

Power Strategies Inc.

Dallas, Texas

Bill my credit card # _____exp._____

Type of card MC AMEX VISA

Signature _____

Book total _____

Postage and handling total_____

Applicable sales tax _____

Total amount due _____

Bill to address_____

City_____

state_____ zip_____

Ship to address_____ city_____

state_____ zip_____

Daytime phone_____ night phone_____

e-mail_____

Please allow four to six weeks for shipping. This offer subject to change.

ABOUT THE AUTHORS

Corporate Team: Unleashing Human Potential

Dr. Ty Talcott

Dr. Ty Talcott

For twenty years Dr. Ty Talcott was a private practicing physician. During this time he had as many as twenty-one employees who he directly managed. His staff and clinic were one of the largest in the country for many years. His staff won dozens of professional awards for outstanding patient care and business performance. The principles in the seminar are the same as were used to coach Dr. Talcott's team.

After Dr. Talcott's retirement from private practice, he became one of the top nine individuals in a multimillion dollar direct sales corporation. During this time, he led a direct sales team and trained tens of thousands of individuals.

Charged with the task of developing his sales force, he was a featured speaker at numerous conventions and the lead trainer at hundreds of seminar events. There is probably no harder industry to excel in than the direct sales industry, but his time and dedication to building his people through "power teams" quickly led him to be invited to record a complete training series for Distributor Services, a division of the world renown Nightingale Conant

Corporation. Nightingale Conant is the world leader in personal development and success principles and represents industry leaders such as Brian Tracey, Stephen Covey, Anthony Robbins, and many more.

Dr. Talcott has also led weekend retreats for start-up businesses for the purpose of developing rock solid A to Z business plans. Due to Dr. Talcott's extensive business experience and success, he was also provided a partnership position in a multimillion dollar real estate development company based in Dallas, Texas. This company has already produced twenty-four subdivisions in the Dallas/Fort Worth area.

Today Dr. Talcott is able to fulfill his lifelong dream of sharing his proven principles, techniques, and strategies allowing all individuals to achieve the highest levels of success through Power Strategies Incorporated. Clients range from corporate groups, to physician associations, to retail chains, sales forces, and any business team that wants to transform to a "power team" to accomplish individual as well as business goals. Visit us at http://www.appliedmotivation.net and see what their clients have to say about the results they obtain from our interactive customized seminars.

Dr. Scott Elliott

Dr. Scott Elliott

As chief operating officer, Dr. Elliott ensures that Power Strategies Inc. maintains the highest level of professional business resources. Dr. Elliott's extensive experience in effectively communicating with individuals from diverse backgrounds and careers, perpetuates the Power Strategies mission to assist a multitude of business entities, organizations, families, and individuals through teaching the science of applied motivation.

Dr. Elliott also has the honor of serving as president of Physicians' Corporation International (PCI) and is responsible for its strategic direction, along with the management and development of company resources. PCI is a corporation that focuses on providing professional income diversification capabilities to doctors, healthcare providers, and business professionals across the United States and is now expanding its efforts internationally into the United Kingdom. The continued success and expansion of PCI is strongly dependent on Dr. Elliott's extensive communication training and experience. PCI is proud to represent doctors from all major fields of practice, as well as business professionals from diverse backgrounds and careers.

Dr. Elliott is passionate about assisting others by ensuring the HIGHEST LEVEL of MANAGEMENT and OPERATIONS of Power Strategies Incorporated.

Printed in the United States
26219LVS00005B/250-282